Echoes
of the
Mekong

Echoes
of the
Mekong

by

Peter A. Huchthausen & Nguyen Thi Lung

Foreword by Sylvana Foa

The Nautical & Aviation Publishing Company of America
Baltimore, Maryland

Library of Congress Catalog Card Number: 95-47725

ISBN: 1-877853-41-0

Printed in the United States of America

Library of Congress Cataloging-In-Publication Data

Huchthausen, Peter A., 1939–
    Echoes of the Mekong / Peter A. Huchthausen & Nguyen Thi Lung.
        p.   cm.
        ISBN 1-877853-41-0
1. Vietnamese Conflict, 1961–1975—Riverine operations, American
2. Vietnamese Conflict, 1961–1975—Personal narratives, American.
3. Huchthausen, Peter A., 1939–   . 4. Nguyen, Thi Lung, 1957–
I. Nguyen, Thi Lung, 1957–   . II.   Title.
DS558.7.H83 1996
959.704′3373—dc20
                                                            95-47725
                                                                CIP

Cover photos official U.S. Navy, courtesy of the U.S. Naval Institute. Illustrations by Christa Huchthausen Mueller. Map by David Bennett.

This is the true story of two people from different cultures whose lives were indelibly marked by war. It is dedicated to those Americans and Vietnamese who lost their lives on the rivers and canals of the Mekong Delta, and especially to the children of the Mekong, who possessed the tenacious resiliance and fierce will to survive.

Contents

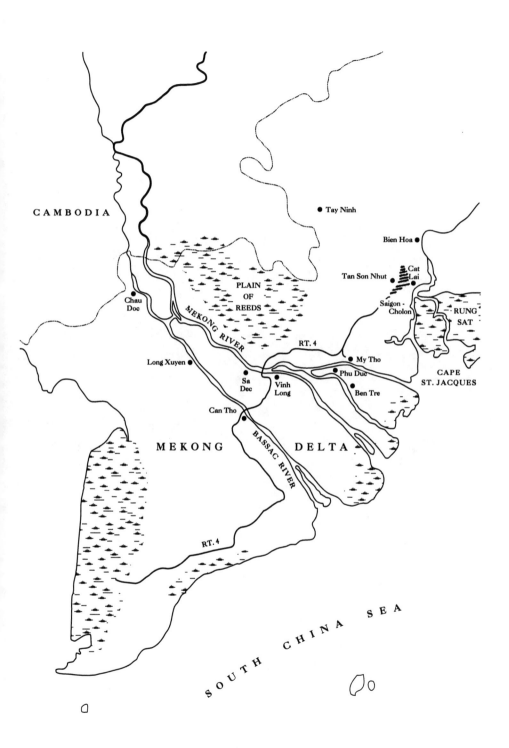

CAMBODIA

Tay Ninh

Bien Hoa

Cat
Lai

Tan Son Nhut

PLAIN
OF
REEDS

Chau
Doc

Saigon -
Cholon

RUNG
SAT

MEKONG RIVER

RT. 4

Long Xuyen

My Tho

CAPE
ST. JACQUES

Sa
Dec

Vinh
Long

Phu Duc

Ben Tre

Can Tho

BASSAC RIVER

MEKONG   DELTA

RT. 4

SOUTH   CHINA   SEA

Foreword

The "beige mice" were everywhere, sticking to us like our sweat-soaked clothes on that hot, steamy April day in Ho Chi Minh City.

As NBC correspondent Neil Davis and I strolled down the street, we nodded to them politely, calling out "Good day Comrade" to the more familiar faces. This enraged the "mice" and they did not return our greetings. It was difficult to maintain decent surveillance on two foreigners surrounded by several dozen chattering children all vying to hold their hands.

Though their uniforms had turned beige with age, these policemen performed their jobs better than the much detested "white mice" who patrolled the same streets and terrorized anyone who dared to dissent in the city then known as Saigon. You knew they were good at their jobs by the fear on the faces of the elderly men and women who darted into the crowd of kids to stuff letters into the oversized pockets of my dress.

The dress was a regular mailbag, as I discovered the first time I wore it. The police might try to confiscate documents put into a foreigner's hands on the grounds they could contain state secrets, but in the crush of people, no one could see the letters disappearing into the folds of my skirt.

Most of the letters were written by the mothers of the youngsters the Vietnamese called "Children of Dust", the Amerasian offspring of U.S. servicemen. They sought help in getting their children added to the Orderly Departure Program (ODP) list that eventually brought tens of thousands of these children to the United States.

Other letters came from former U.S. government employees released from re-education camps, asking their American friends to honor promises made six years earlier to not forget or abandon them.

On that particular day, one letter stood out. Addressed to the U.S. Embassy in Bangkok, it contained a much-folded photograph of a little Vietnamese girl and two young Americans. The heartbreaking story it told pushed me to break my own rule and I wrote a story about it upon my return to the UPI (United Press International) office in Bangkok.

"Do you remember little Huynh Thi Lung?" the story began. "She remembers you."

Hal Foster, then Editor-in-Chief of *Pacific Stars and Stripes*, called minutes after the story hit the wire to tell me it was making the front page. About a week later, Hal called again, this time to tell me that a Captain Peter Huchthausen, then serving as the U.S. Naval Attaché in Belgrade, had contacted him after friends of his identified him as the dashing Navy lieutenant in Lung's photo. Furthermore, Captain Huchthausen wanted to sponsor Lung and her daughter for the Orderly Departure Program. It was 1981.

The ODP procedures were complicated. Relations between the United States and Vietnam were not amicable and the American authorities were inundated with applications for ODP, many of them fraudulent.

I called the U.S. Embassy regularly for an update on Lung's case. I wanted to write the "happy ending", and because Lung's case did not fit neatly into any of the traditional ODP categories, I did not want some bureaucrat to dump it in the reject pile. Luckily, Lung's case was handled by some of the most caring people I have ever met. But even for them, the red tape was formidable.

In 1982, UPI transferred me to Hong Kong to serve as Asia/Pacific News Editor, but I could not forget the heartrending tale told in Lung's letter.

One day in 1984, I got a call from friends at the U.S. Embassy in Bangkok. "You can get off our backs," they laughed. "She's on her way."

But not really. She and her daughter only travelled as far as a desolate, dusty ODP transit camp in the Philippines. There she awaited final clearance to travel to the United States.

Though advised not to contact her in Vietnam as it might cause her difficulties, as soon as I heard she was in the Philippines, I hopped on a plane and went to find her. Our visit was brief and with no common language, we had great difficulty communicating. The months and months of waiting and the misery of the transit camp had taken a terrible toll. She was at the end of her rope.

Captain Huchthausen and I spoke again and more pressure was put on the authorities to speed up her case. It seemed to take forever.

In the end, there was a "happy ending", although I did not get to write it. The two people who *did* remember each other after all those years, have written it themselves.

Sylvana Foa
Spokesman for the Secretary
General of the United Nations

Chapter I

The Village

Lung

The late evening breeze finally nudged away the day's heat and pushed the mosquitoes back to the marshes hidden deep in the Mekong Delta. It was the golden time of day, I thought, a time when everything was at its best. The oppressive heat and dust were gone, the irritation and discomfort cleansed by the breeze. The cool expanse of the nearby river eased my fears of distant guns as darkness enveloped everything around me.

I lay on my straw mat on a ledge in our thatch-covered home by a canal leading to the main river. My five brothers feared the night, but at age ten, I loved soft light and shadows. My name, Lung, means short. But in the dark I was no longer smaller or weaker than my brothers. In the evenings my voice rivaled theirs. I was not little, at least not in heart.

The next day I would cover a long distance on the wonderful river. The flowing waters made me feel stronger and bolder by concealing my size. On the river I moved as fast as my brothers, steered a sampan as accurately as the others, and moved as nimbly as they between bobbing boats. I never fell in the water, unless I wanted to. I knew there was too much work to permit play, but I played secretly while we worked. I enjoyed picking the squash and gathering the garlic and tying up the bundles of greens for the market. When I carried fish sauce cans to the loading pier from the gigantic vat under the corrugated roof of the nuc mam building, I was carrying imaginary bricks to build my house.

The fish and crab were my companions in the maze of canals connecting our village of Phu Duc with the other hamlets lining the broad Mekong. The river at that point is called Cu Long, meaning "nine dragons" for the nine separate channels which heave the river's gathered riches into the sea. Actually, there were only eight channels—one silted up many years ago—but nine is a preferred number to Vietnamese. The wealth of rich topsoil and fish are mixed with the residue of human suffering during the river's long meander from the Himalayas to the South China Sea. We grew to know that suffering first hand.

In the morning I would travel by water taxi from our village to the market in the grand town of My Tho. After tomorrow I would rival my older brother, Cao, who made the trip often, by carrying my own load of fruit to sell and returning with the goods all sold, and a pocket full of *dong* to prove my success. I watched the glitter of stars through the gaps in the grass roof, confident I was as strong as my brothers, and maybe smarter. They did not know a thing about cooking or working inside our small home as I did, yet I could perform many of their chores with ease and grace.

A wave of warmth surged through me, and I wondered why I felt so sure everything would be different after the next day's trip. I somehow knew it would be, just as I knew that dreams seen in succession often come true. It had happened to me before, after seeing the same dream three times. It was as unfailing as the sun, and as predictable as the river current.

The river and sun were my special signs of safety and comfort. When guns sounded in the distance, then closer, the nearness of the river and the presence of the sun reduced my fears. The gun sounds had become more frequent, but were still seldom heard nearby. Once I heard rapid shooting from the river near the village. The noise frightened me, but that rarely happened in daylight.

The clatter of shooting was always accompanied by a visit from the government's foot soldiers. Those miserable figures would sweep through the village and surrounding fields only in daytime, carrying weapons too heavy for their size. They seldom succeeded in finding or confronting the Vietcong. In any case, it was wise to keep away from them. Sometimes traps or mines set by the Vietcong exploded, horribly wounding the young South Vietnamese soldiers who walked with frightened eyes along the village paths and through the rice fields.

The round metal hats the soldiers wore made them look ridiculous—they were much too large. The helmets often fell over their eyes, forcing the soldiers to hold their heads at absurd angles in order to see. When these men were nearby it was good to keep chickens and ducks hidden to keep them alive. It was best, in all cases, to hide when the soldiers came through.

The Vietcong were different. They moved only at night, and seemed to glide without noise. But it was dangerous too when they came. Life for the people in our village was a delicate balance between opposing forces. To live safely we needed to tread gently. Like the river, the village balanced conflicting forces of affection and danger. Despite the fear and danger, I was happy.

I hugged myself as I thought about tomorrow's trip. I would meet cousin Din at the river station. We would travel together on the river, and its waters would protect us. Together Din and I were strong, like the heroic Trung sisters of early Vietnamese history. Together we imagined ourselves as the fearless Trung Trac and her sister Trung Nhi in ancient Vietnam who had raised an army and led a campaign against the invading Chinese. The two victorious sisters had founded a kingdom. They were the first successful leaders in a long series of Vietnamese uprisings against the Chinese.

That night my thoughts drifted off to the rice fields and embankments stretching out from the quiet village, along the canal, past the fish stakes which stood like crooked fingers in the shallows. I imagined myself floating above the dark sampans bobbing empty along the banks and gently chafing against one another. I floated out to the Cu Long, where stars reflected their shimmering light on the black moving waters. The faint smell of nuc mam faded into the night breeze. The air was sweet like the scent of the mango as it made a rhythmic brushing sound on the high grass along the edge of the village.

Drifting near sleep, I was suddenly awakened as the sound of the wind in the grass was transformed into muffled footsteps. I listened as they came again, louder. The whispering breeze which had lulled me to sleep earlier now mingled with the sound of excited voices. I lay fully awake, but did not move. Not tonight, I thought, on my special night. I waited, trying not to breathe. Again, silence. Maybe it was my imagination. The quiet pressed in on me. Suddenly a rattle, more muffled steps, and stifled whispers. No, I thought. Please not now. I wished the intruders would pass by.

I raised my head and peered through a crack in the wall toward the center of the village. Darting flames split the darkness. Flickering lights moved at shoulder height. First one torch danced in the night, then several appeared, carried by ghost-like figures.

I covered my ears at the sound of metal against metal. The steady beat woke the sleeping villagers. I put my ear against the wall and heard the chilling announcement that made my flesh tighten: "Awaken villagers. Gather to meet those who depend on your sustenance."

I loathed these night visits. My chest tightened as I remembered the last visit several months ago. I knew the intruders expected us to file out of the house together, sit in a semicircle around the torches and listen to the Vietcong fables. It was too dangerous to resist. Mother said one should not tease an angry tiger, or torment a wounded water buffalo. The Vietcong were swift and vicious. I had heard the stories of villagers who defied the night cadres. An elder from a nearby village once had his head severed from his body in front of a similar night gathering. It had happened but months ago. Everyone knew about it, but tried to ignore the memory.

I heard my mother stir. She called softly to wake my brother. I sat up and waited. Would I have to go? I still looked young enough to remain in bed. She came to the side of the straw mat, looked down at me quietly, and put her cold hand on my shoulder. My three younger brothers slept peacefully in the far corner of the hut. "Come Lung, you too must attend. They'll find you if you do not go."

I rose in silence and pulled on my cotton smock, pleased in a way that I was considered important enough to go. Together the three of us filed quietly out of the hut, and walked slowly to the center of the hamlet. We encountered the startled faces of other villagers similarly wrenched from their slumber. Apprehension showed in their faces, made even more frightening by the flickering torchlight which cast strange shadows on their bleary features. Two figures in black directed the stumbling people to sit in a semicircle. The intruders neither spoke nor smiled. They merely pointed, gently steering the drowsy citizens who moved like complacent animals and sat where directed.

The crowd at the center of the village grew until it included more than one hundred huddled, wide-eyed inhabitants. Suddenly, two more guards stepped forward from the encircling torchlight, their arms linked to a man between them. A gasp went up from the crowd as the villagers recognized the quivering figure. He was the Phu Duc village chief, an older man I knew to be in his mid-sixties and already frail. His knees were bent and his head bowed. Poor man; he was not a good speaker at such gatherings. Appointed to the position by the Ben Tre Province chief and in the village less than a year, he was an outsider, not from Phu Duc.

The last chief of Phu Duc, a popular and highly respected man, had disappeared on a night similar to this. Although a local rice-farmer and both widely known and admired, it did not help him when he dared to stand and speak his mind during a Vietcong rally. I heard him tell the assembly that it was the right of the people to choose their own leaders, their own system, and their own way of life. He had permission to speak at the gathering, but was later attacked verbally by Vietcong leaders who called him a puppet of

Saigon and a slave of the foreigners. After the rally, the village chief disappeared. I remembered him as a kind man: a man of conviction. His family quietly moved away following his disappearance.

I sat next to my mother and brother and watched in silence. The new village chief was pulled to the front of the crowd. An older man dressed in black, shouldered his way out of the darkness, and looked sternly at the silent crowd.

"Greetings, people of the village of Phu Duc," he said. "We want you to join the great crusade for the unity of Vietnam, the purging of the degenerate puppets of foreign colonials, and the freeing of all Vietnamese. We hope you will join us and become the willing sea that surrounds and nurtures the fish of the action squads of the revolution, the vanguard of the proletariate."

I had difficulty following the logic of the speech. It did not all make sense. If they were here to help the village, why did they awaken everyone in the middle of the night, when we wanted to sleep?

I watched the speaker stride back and forth as he addressed the crowd. "Recall the great thirteenth century Vietnamese general, Tran Hung Dao, father of guerrilla warfare. He trained an army like the Vietcong to rise up against the numerically superior invaders the Mongols, led by Kublai Khan. Today, we again fight an enemy who occupies our Vietnam; again foreigners want to enslave you in your own land."

He pointed at the crowd, which stared back intently. Despite the fact that we were all southerners, it was inspirational to hear how the venerated general, Tran Hung Dao, defeated the Mongols in the north. He did so, according to the Vietcong speaker, by the application of superior knowledge of the local terrain, and the cunning use of the rivers, rice fields, canals, and hills. Using the local farmer's intimate knowledge of the area, the patriot army had overwhelmed the enemy.

The speaker walked forward and put his hands on the shoulders of one villager and said, "As in the past, your patriotic duty is to support the guerrilla fighters, who, like the ancient fighters under Tran Hung Dao, will purge the country of the foreign invaders and those Vietnamese traitors who support them. We will then free the country to unite and flourish on the riches of the land now being wasted in this struggle."

I looked around at the others in the crowd. They appeared spellbound. The speaker was convincing: he was clever and captivated the throng with tales of the Mongols using detailed episodes to illustrate the story of the final stand against the Mongols at the river Bach Dang. Using tactics learned from even earlier Vietnamese history, the peasant-soldiers placed pointed stakes in the mud under the surface of the river waters to puncture and sink attacking Mongol boats. The speaker emphasized the personal role of each person in supporting an army of mobile resistance fighters. The advantage of the peasant army lay in its ability to fade unseen into the surrounding villages and disappear into the sea of supporting followers.

The lecturer painted a vivid picture for the people of Phu Duc, whose lives were so closely entwined with the river that they shared a natural identity with the stories. The people were easily swayed by the promise of improved life and quickly intimidated by the threat of force. The Vietcong leader aimed his rhetoric at the weak points in the structure of the villagers' lives. In this case, the focus was on the appointment of an outsider as our village chief, a man the villagers neither trusted nor respected.

The speech had gone on for what seemed like hours when finally I heard, "Get up off the ground! Stand up people of Phu Duc! Each family will let two of our soldiers sleep in your homes the next time we come calling to your village." The speaker glared at the two men who had held the chief between them throughout the long speech. The men released their hold on the new village chief and roughly pushed him forward. He fell to his knees in front of the crowd. In a weak voice he implored, "People of Phu Duc, you must volunteer your homes to billet and feed two soldiers each." His voice rose to a shrill and unsteady tone as he assured, "No harm will come to those who cooperate, and there will be rewards to those who help the guerrilla army to victory." Several villagers stepped forward and, taking a pen offered by a soldier, made their marks in a small book held by another soldier. I thought they signed just to be allowed to return to their homes and to get back to sleep.

It was strange, I thought, that none of the black-clad Vietcong carried weapons into the village. They were polite yet firm. They seemed harmless. I wondered why everyone was so frightened. More people signed their names and returned to their homes. The scene in the center of the village was calm. The speaker had been soft-spoken and pleasant, and exuded a sense of purpose, strength, and fairness. But the scene around the outer perimeter of the village was totally different.

I followed my mother as she went forward to make a mark in the book. Starting back toward the hut, I walked on tiptoes in order to look beyond the houses. I saw a group of Vietcong, perhaps twenty or more, loitering behind the line of houses. As we walked toward our hut in the flickering torchlight, I noticed a group of young village men standing in a row behind the houses. A low but excited chatter came from the area. I suddenly recognized my fourteen-year-old brother, Cao, standing in the row of men.

The Vietcong soldiers who gathered around the small group appeared different from the leaders who had herded the citizens to the middle of the village. I noted that these agile-looking figures carried weapons—guns and rocket launchers. Many of the black figures wore khaki bands of ammunition and checkered scarves; some carried long knives. I turned to look more closely and noticed that their feet looked hard and worn in their home-made sandals. I looked up and saw that their hair was cropped short, their noses flat. Their dark faces had fierce looks. Several bore scars. Not one was heavy or fat.

Three older and armed Vietcong slowly worked their way down the front of the line. They looked at each young man and after a brief exchange of words, either pushed him over to another group standing to the side, or left him standing in the line. Armed men carrying long tube-like weapons with rockets, surrounded those culled out.

I stumbled along and saw that the young villagers behind the house were tied together with a long rope. They looked at the ground with heads bowed, offering no resistance. Then to one side I saw a young man on the ground. I stared at the form. I did not recognize the person because only his head and back were visible, but I noticed how strangely he was lying on the ground, flat as if hugging the earth. In the torchlight I could see a pool of blood spreading around his head and neck; the light reflected from the pool of black liquid.

My mother pulled at my arm and led me away. We entered our dark house. I climbed back onto my straw bed, huddled down into the covers, and tried to erase the dancing torches from my mind. Despite the effort, I kept seeing the figure of the boy on the ground. I curled up into a tight ball, terrified that my older brother might be put in the line of men tied together like animals.

Finally I heard my mother sigh in relief as my older brother walked in, looking dazed. "They're gone," he whispered. "They said I was too young and weak." For a moment he looked disappointed and dejected. Mother put her arm on his shoulder and I could see the relief on her face for this mixed blessing: although the rejection was humiliating, there was relief that he was not taken. Mother said nothing and pushed him onto his mat in the corner of the hut.

I closed my eyes, but continued to see the young man lying in the dirt. I tried to push the image away, and finally drifted off to sleep. I dreamed in a recurring nightmare that my older brother lay on the ground, then my next brother, and then the next—each of them surrounded by a glimmering pool of dark blood.

Chapter II

River Sailors

Peter

The night was partially cloudy and moonless. The dark sky merged with the ebony treeline of the riverbanks, which in turn blended with the ink-black water of the river. Two heavily-armed river patrol boats drifted in silence less than fifty yards from the south bank, and near the point where the Cua Tieu and the Ham Luong branches split. A single canal entered the main river one hundred meters west of this point. Along with the other hushed sailors of the crew, I stared in the direction of the canal mouth until my eyes began to burn. I peered through a night observation device called a starlight scope, which enabled an observer to see movement using a passive system generated by background light. The only sound was the sporadic lapping of water against the fiber glass hulls of the boats and the wash against the distant riverbank. Nothing moved except the river, which flowed with a pleasant hiss. I adjusted the scope with a slight turn of a knob, my thoughts drifting with the water.

Like the Vietnamese in the delta, the American river sailors had learned to love the Mekong. Here the river was sovereign. Like an empress, the river ruled over all; from the beginning of her 2,600 mile plunge in the Himalayan Mountains in central Tibet, through Yunnan Province of China, she carved the border between Laos, Burma, and then Thailand, sliced through Cambodia, and then sprawled into two swollen arms and entered Vietnam.

I felt a tug on my arm. "See anything, Skipper?" It was the coxswain, Henderson, whispering hoarsely in the blackness.

"No. We'll wait another half-hour."

My thoughts returned to the vast delta that encompassed most of Vietnam below Saigon. Nourished by the rich topsoil swept out of the lands traversed by the Mekong, the delta forms a wealthy rice bowl capable of feeding all of Asia, were the farming left uninterrupted by war.

The American sailors loved the Mekong, but they were not her masters. They knew her winding course, tributaries, mouth, and back waters. They knew of her shallows and of the invisible fish stakes. They were protective of her sampan traffic and her thousands of children, though one in ten had been killed or wounded in the last ten years of conflict.

The delta people, one-fifth of the population of Vietnam, transport nearly one hundred percent of the fruits of their labor on the veins and arteries of the waterways. The river's breadth was a refuge, her darkness and current an ally for both sides. But her overgrown banks were feared and the intertwining canals tested the bravest man's courage. I thought of my crews who, despite their boldness, grew to respect those feared canals, where the enemy lay concealed and well entrenched.

Our ten river patrol boats, called PBRs, were virtually impervious to the enemy while on the main rivers. In open space, maneuverability and firepower rendered them difficult targets. But in the canals, the advantage shifted to a wily enemy concealed in the natural brush and protected by the high banks. Under the rules of engagement, we could only return fire when fired upon unless the enemy could be visually identified. That gave the enemy the luxury of choosing when and where to engage. Under those rules, our advantage in firepower was whittled away to an uneasy parity with the Vietcong. In combat action on the rivers and canals, victory could go to either side, and was generally determined by the degree of surprise achieved by one or the other.

One day earlier, an army intelligence cell had reported to the two American river patrol sections based in My Tho that the Vietcong had recently been crossing the river at the junction of the Ham Luong and Cua Tieu. Previous sightings by night patrols confirmed that sampans had ventured out from the same canal and attempted to cross the main river after curfew. Vietcong couriers and assault teams often used the river at night, while we did our best to catch them. Our two boats now waited tensely in the early hours of the morning.

"Skipper, first light is in a couple of hours. Should we keep drifting?"

I peered through the scope at the green outline of the trees on the bank. The hours of drifting downstream and countless scans of the bank, had produced nothing. But at the closest point of approach, the outline of two forms gradually took shape in the green image of the scope. I did not answer, but blinked several times and looked again. There was abrupt and clear movement. In the surreal setting, the outlines of two small sampans moved slowly from the mouth of the canal and poked their bows into the main river. A blur of motion on each sampan indicated at least one, possibly two people paddling. There was no sound.

I lowered the scope, grabbed the VHF radio hand set, and keyed the mike twice, alerting the cover boat. No one spoke. I reached down from the canopy and groped for the boat captain, Bob Gallagher. I felt the sailor's flak jacket, squeezed his upper arm, and pointed with a nod toward the bank. I passed the scope to Gallagher and stepped down from the engine cover to alert the coxswain.

Darkness hid both the bank and the enemy, but knowledge of their proximity made the air electric. They too were straining to make out our forms, and each side waited for a tell-tale noise, a flicker of light, or a reflection upon which to train a weapon. A sudden panic seized me, and I fought the urge to quickly do something, anything, to preempt the rising fear.

Four sharp cracks abruptly shattered the silence and debris flew past my ear. Then silence, as we momentarily froze with the shock of the firing. That split-second return to silence seemed to stretch into minutes as I motioned to coxswain Henderson to start the engines. Instead, the young third class bo'sun mate slumped against the thin steel armor of the coxswain's compartment, his arms crossed, squeezing his shoulders.

"I'm hit, Sir," he whispered. I moved quickly to support his body, guiding him to the engine cover, and pushing him down into a sitting position. I stepped into the coxswain's position and reached for the engine starter.

"Let's go," I said softly into the hand mike. We had to start moving even if the noise disclosed our positions. As I reached for the starter button, my mind raced. The sniper surely had some sort of night observation device, since it was totally black on the river. We had made no noise, there were no silhouettes. How the hell could they see us? I wondered, as I found the rubber encased starter button and pressed. The horn sounded in a short beep, echoing out over the black river.

"Shit." My thumb instinctively found the adjacent and identical button. A deafening roar erupted as the twin diesel engines exploded to life. I pushed the double throttles to full forward, and the boat lurched ahead and sped away into the blackness.

The cover boat followed immediately. A short burst followed from the riverbank, throwing green tracers at us. The tracers marked the target, and the forward gunner automatically swung his twin 50-caliber machine gun mount toward the flashes on the bank.

"Take the helm, Gallagher. There are two sampans moving in the canal." I left the coxswain's position and turned to the wounded bo'sun, still leaning forward on the engine cover, clutching his shoulders.

"Hang in there, Henderson." I peeled the hunched figure's hands away, removed his flak jacket, and examined his shoulder in the beam of a red-lensed flashlight. I found a neat hole near the base of his neck, and another, much bigger hole in his biceps. Pink flesh poked through a nasty gash three inches wide. The bullet had exited, leaving a dirty wound with splintered bones and torn tendons inside. There was little blood, probably due to shock, I thought.

I spoke again into the radio mike. "Delta-five, delta-five," thus directing the boats into a racetrack pattern offset from the canal entrance, the apparent source of the shooters. I leaned forward, tapped the bow gunner, and stabbed my finger in the direction of the canal opening. "There to the left," I shouted above the engine whine. The gunner slipped the safety off the twin 50s.

"Make a run past the canal entrance, two sampans trying to cross. The shits saw us," I shouted to Gallagher and simultaneously into the mike. I grabbed for support as the boat pitched ahead at full speed.

"Got you covered Skipper," came the voice over the speakers as the cover boat took position fifty yards astern, the white rooster tail of wake now visible to the naked eye.

I tapped the forward gunner hard on the shoulder. "Put in some short bursts—there, just off the bow." The command was followed by a loud staccato popping as red tracer fire penetrated the darkness in terrifying torrents. The gunner continued to fire into the bank, and the tracer streams increased as the cover boat joined.

Only seconds had passed since the sniper began shooting. No doubt the gunfire had originated from a Vietcong team covering the sampan crossing. The tracer rounds formed colorful lines of light as they extended from each boat, arched high into the dark sky, and ricochetted off the treeline. Despite the bright firepower display, the darkness of the riverbank hid a cold picture of death.

I turned back to Henderson, now huddled on the engine cover, and quickly wrapped a battle dressing tight around his wounds. "How's he doin' Sir?" Gallagher asked. I lowered the bo'sun full length onto the engine cover and wrapped a poncho around him for warmth.

"I'm not sure. He's not bleeding much—probably still in shock. Make another run," I shouted, and began sending a series of three-letter radio codes to the operations center in My Tho. I gave our position and reported that we were under fire—although that should have been obvious to anyone listening in on a receiver.

"Damn your night vision, you bastards," I muttered in frustration as I selected an M-79 grenade launcher from the gun locker. I tore off the safety and leaned against the canopy supports. As the boats again approached the canal mouth, barely visible as a slight difference in shade of black from the treeline, I fired a single round toward the riverbank.

The grenade launcher was a handy weapon at night. Fired from the hip in darkness, when sighting was futile, it was remarkably accurate. The round exploded with a flash, briefly lighting the area. I reached for a flare gun and slipped a round into it. A loud burst of static on the radio caught my attention as a voice began repeating another series of three-letter codes.

"Take this and illuminate the canal," I shouted between the deafening bursts of the forward guns, and handed the flare gun to Gallagher. He was still on the helm, but able to raise the flare projector from under the canopy and fire it high in the direction of the bank. I held the red-lensed flashlight on the menu board attached to the armored plate next to the radios, and read off the meaning of the codes coming in from the speakers.

"Cease fire, your rounds are hitting a friendly outpost in Ham Luong a kilometer behind the treeline. Cease fire," the message read. I watched the flare burst over the riverbank and bathe the entire treeline and bank in a ghostly white light. I motioned Gallagher to continue the circuit around again, and peered with binoculars into the canal mouth which now appeared as clear as day in the flare light.

"Nothing there anymore. Crap. Check fire, check fire." I repeated the command over the radio. The two boats continued around as a second flare from the cover boat burst over the area. There was nothing visible in the canal. The crossing had been aborted.

"Head for Dong Tam," I shouted to Gallagher over the engine whine. I picked up the mike again and gave instructions to the cover boat. "Stay in the area, keep moving and watch the canal until relieved. We're taking wounded into Dong Tam." The ops center would copy the message simultaneously, so I hung up the mike and turned again to the wounded Henderson lying on the engine cover. A small pool of blood had formed and was running down the side of the compartment onto the deck. I examined his wounds again, adjusted the battle dressing, and tried to talk to the sailor. The sound of the engines drowned out my words. The boat screamed on at top speed toward the Dong Tam base and the aid station located on a floating pier.

"How long to Dong Tam?" I leaned forward to get closer to Gallagher.

"It'll take about thirty minutes to get there, Boss."

A good start, I thought. It was my first time out alone as patrol officer. I had been on three indoctrination patrols with other officers, once with commanding officer Lieutenant Lowell Webb. The other patrols had each been with different chief petty officers, who were also patrol officers, one to every two-boat patrol.

The PBR made its way toward the brightly lit floating aid station. The crew jumped to mooring stations as I helped hand the wounded Henderson to the medics. "Two holes, in the neck and shoulder. Single round of small arms, no drugs, lost minimal blood," I called to the medics who moved quickly to prepare the wounded bo'sun for evacuation. The forms moved like dancers in the bright light, accompanied by the roar of the diesel engines and the familiar *thwock, thwock* of a medevac helicopter.

"Clear the barge. Helo inbound with casualties. Clear the area," someone shouted with authority.

"Gallagher, go with Henderson. We'll send someone back for you later. Call in when you get a chance." I took the controls, cast off from the float, and started back through the large side canal. The small boat answered my grip on the controls as we headed for the main river and My Tho.

I watched as the first tinge of a grey dawn spread off to the east. The early morning river breeze was cold and I pulled my flak jacket together and fastened it around me for warmth. I looked down and noticed the jacket was covered with blood—not my blood, but Henderson's, one of my own men. As I looked down, my hand began to shake and for the first time, I became acutely aware of the awesome responsibility of command. I shuddered, realizing that the decisions I had made had resulted in casualties and I suddenly felt very alone. This responsibility was more potent than I had ever imagined and I felt stupid remembering how I blew the horn instead of hitting the start button. As the boat raced on my thoughts drifted back to the long period of preparation and training at Mare Island and in San Diego before I arrived in the delta town of My Tho to join the river patrol section as the second in command.

Training

A ragged formation of olive-drab figures swayed in unison as it snaked down the hill toward the shipyard in the foggy morning air. A muttered cadence came in short barks from the chief bo'sun as the thud of boots on wet pavement pounded out their own muffled rhythm. Few commands were necessary.

"Hey," clump. "Ho," clump. Down the winding road, in quiet but solid harmony, forty heaving figures lost in private thoughts allowed the cadence of their boots to lull them into a trance punctuated only by the odd grunt or wheeze as they jogged easily down the hill. "Hey," clump, clump, clump. "Ho," clump, clump, clump. The platoon descended through the haze from the isolation of the grey stone barracks, into the familiar shipyard filled with the accustomed sights and smells they chose to leave behind.

"Close it up, Lieutenant," called the chief bo'sun, as the knot of puffing figures clumped across the asphalt. "You goddamn officers got to keep up to the rest of us," he murmured just loudly enough for the front rank of the formation to hear. I panted heavily, in the second rank behind the guide, still disliking the early morning runs.

Like two others in the platoon, I had just come from a destroyer where I served as the engineering officer. For the past week the river patrol training platoon had been getting up at four o'clock each morning for pre-breakfast calisthenics and a two-mile run. It was not the toughness of the drill that hurt, but the humiliation. The officers were accustomed to slightly more delicate treatment, but we gamely overlooked the odd phenomenon of hazing by older, senior petty officers with many more years in the fleet.

We ran in cadence over the wet pavement of the shipyard where the morning shift of sullen civilian shipyard workers, called "crabs" by the sailors, had not yet poured through the gates. Like most sailors, I associated shipyards with discomfort, noise, and the nuisance of the occasional overhaul of our revered ships. Hard-hat crabs, usually a bunch of thoughtless landlubbers, violated the very soul of a ship by forcing the exposure of the hull, a vulnerable and sacred portion of the ship. Gleaming pump rooms, spotless engine rooms and machinery spaces, the hallowed pilot house, pristine signal bridge, and immaculate mess decks—the prized results of round-the-clock cleanliness and maintenance accomplished during long weeks and months at sea—all were violated in the yard by the shipyard "crabs."

In the distance, below the hill, the form of a destroyer deck gradually took shape in the mist. The figures of the four-to-eight quarterdeck watch stood like wooden dolls, barely visible in the glow from a single light that illuminated the grey ship. As I puffed up and down hills with the other fleet escapees—volunteers for duty in the little-known river patrol force, destined for assignment to the backwaters of the Mekong River—I realized there would be no more endless one-in-three watches, four hours on, eight off, week after week, month after month.

The grey hull of the destroyer loomed in the mist, connnected to the pier by rows of electrical cables, steam lines, and welding leads. Like multiple umbilical cords, they provided the vital energy for life normally supplied by the ship's own engineering plant. A cloud of hissing steam rose from the pier-side manifolds where the electrical lines replacing the destroyer's silent auxiliary plant snaked aboard. The canvas covering the dented smoke stacks indicated that the steam plants, so lovingly maintained by the ship's engineers for so many miles, now lay silent, her gleaming turbines resting on bowed shafts, cold and dead. The four mighty 600-psi steam boilers, formerly the prized possessions of grimy boiler tenders, lay in similar neglect. The boiler tenders were both caring and fiercely protective of their equipment, the pumps and valves which now lay in gutted atrophy deep in the firerooms, whose deckplates were once clean enough to eat from—the boiler tenders favorite boast.

A pang of nostalgia ran through me as our formation ran past the ship. The quarter-deck watch stared as we trotted down the wet pier. "Let's hear it—PBR," shouted the cheif bo'sun as he turned and jogged backwards with the formation. The formation began a rhythmic chant: "PBRs get all the pay, get the tincans out' the way, PBRs roll through the muck, while the tincan sailors suck."

The handful of sailors on the main deck gawked in silence as the formation swung by, turned at the head of the pier, and began the run back toward the hill. Suddenly, one sailor on the ship, holding a coffee cup in one hand, swung out his other arm in a familiar gesture of obscenity and shouted, "You'll get yours, you little shits."

*   *   *

The three months of preparation for Vietnam river duty, consisting of a syllabus of varied courses, was nearly complete. Survival, escape, and evasion training consisted of seven days of semi-starvation, trekking through the wilds of the Warner Springs, California woods and desert. Night marches followed evasion from imaginary enemy capture exercises, including sweat boxes, hours of isolation, reprieve, interrogation, physical beating, and mental hazing. When the flesh is weak from reduced food intake, the mind lags and caves in to make-believe situations. All of us in the survival and evasion training course knew full well our problems would end after seven days, and that the cadre of enemy forces were merely other sailors playing the game. Despite prior warning that submission to the mock interrogation by the trainers would result in a forced repeat of the course, some students still broke. With the gradual wearing down of the body by sleep deprivation, the mental capacity of the young men began to wear away. Confronting six fierce soldiers who directed mock rage against one individual trainee at a time, in a closed room with physical contact authorized, a mild slapping around resulted in submission by a surprising number of the young trainees. Concentrated yet minor brutality by the cadre had defeated some inductees who lacked the spirit vital to a cohesive fighting unit. This lesson was seared into the minds of officers and petty officers alike: an enemy unhampered by restraints on physical abuse could achieve a great deal more. This was perhaps the most valuable training meted out to the future fighters. The training had frightened many, broken some, and caused sobering self-criticism in others.

Many participants in this phase of training were Navy carrier pilots who later found themselves in interment camps in North Vietnam. Most praised the survival training; others said it had not been harsh enough. None regretted the preparation. Emerging from the week of physical abuse, ten pounds lighter, ravenously hungry yet unable to eat the bowl of steaming oatmeal thrust before us, we felt delivered but shaken by the experience. Sobered and motivated, we left determined never to face an armed enemy as a helpless captive.

The training included diesel engine and jacuzzi propulsion pump maintenance, small arms training, river tactics, and combat first aid. These courses were interspersed with indoctrination lectures on the history of the conflict in Vietnam and with noble attempts to teach a group of crusty senior petty officers and junior officers, fresh from fleet destroyers or amphibious ships, the nuances of Vietnamese culture. Trainees were told never to display the soles of their feet to the Vietnamese, never to point directly at a Vietnamese, and not to shout when not understood the first time when addressing a Vietnamese. Nine weeks of intense Vietnamese language followed, which most of the sailors flunked outright despite the efforts of several delicate young Vietnamese language instructors.

The Vietnamese language is not terribly difficult. Its written form is in Roman script called quoc ngu, rather than the Chinese ideograms, thanks to the Portugese Jesuit missionaries in Vietnam in the seventeenth century. The French colonials made quoc ngu and French the official languages in the nineteenth century, thus delivering the Vietnamese from the burden of memorizing the traditional, complex Chinese ideograms. The language is pronounced exactly as written. The fact it was a tonal language, wherein one word could have as many as six different meanings depending on the accent or ending lilt, was for the most part lost on the sailors. The practical bluejackets, however, soon mastered enough words and phrases for survival on the rivers and achieved a remarkable grasp of Vietnamese slang, which they used with surprising effectiveness, especially when combined with a liberal dose of sign language.

The final three weeks of preparation took place on the river patrol boats at Mare Island, California. We first met the boats, nicknamed PBRs, in the fetid backwaters of the Sacramento River, northeast of the San Francisco Bay. We were housed in the bachelor quarters at the Mare Island shipyard, a freezing, white-knuckle, ninety minute boat run under the Martinez-Benecia Bridge, past the ghost-like forms of the mothballed merchant reserve fleet to the sloughs of Suisun Bay. These meandering waterways were topographically similar to the rivers and canals of the Vietnamese

Mekong Delta. However, in February the temperature hovered near freezing, a good fifty degrees lower than in the Mekong. But details never interfered with purposeful navy training.

The three weeks at Mare Island were spiced with reality by the presence of two chief petty officers just returning from duty in the river patrol force. Oddly enough, while these veterans should have enriched the training with their first-hand experiences, they were only heard from indirectly and seldom seen. They were referred to by the instructors as "veteran rats," and were the source of many cryptic rules. When rational explanation escaped the instructors, their logic was attributed to the returned veterans. One veteran, hopelessly shell-shocked, had been in several terrible ambushes and lost nearly his entire crew. The second was a sullen chief engineman who, when coherent, dwelt only on the serious lack of spare parts for the boats in Vietnam. Both veterans were seen mostly in the chiefs' club at the shipyard, usually in the advanced stages of inebriation, surrounded by eager sailors listening to war stories. The navy had somehow failed to recruit one single skilled and motivated survivor of a year in Vietnam to lend a sense of realism to the training for the outgoing river patrol sailors, all sorely in need of an injection of esprit de corps.

The PBR, or patrol boat river in navy jargon, was a fiberglass, thirty-one foot converted pleasure craft with twin General Motors 220-hp diesel engines powering two jacuzzi water pumps, which propelled the boat at remarkably high speeds. This was achieved by virtually thrusting water through directional nozzles, allowing travel through shallow waters with no risk of damaging propellers or rudders. Fully loaded, the boats could skim along at twenty-five to thirty knots in as little as eighteen inches of water. They were perfect platforms for operating in the shallow brown waters of the Mekong River Delta.

The PBRs unique engine whine and still more unusual handling characteristics set them apart from the more conventional and less dashing river craft. A PBR handled so well at high speed that the slightest touch of the helm caused immediate and violent reaction. At slow speeds it was an obstinate beast. Successfully handling the PBR at lower speeds required the coxswain to turn the helm exactly opposite than would be done in a normal boat because of the reverse effect of the nozzles. Thus, most sailors chose to bring a PBR into berth at high speed with a minimum of engine maneuvers, which caused most dockings to become spectacular displays of daring. If done well, such maneuvers were called skillful seamanship. If not done with precision, the resulting crunch often required a hefty fiberglass repair job.

Since many PBR characteristics were the opposite of those of other small boats, these maneuvers could be learned only by experience. Nevertheless, the ardent small craft handler could learn in short order to set these bundles of energy smartly alongside a pier, even against the strong river current. To dock while heading downstream was nearly impossible and usually resulted in an uncontrollable yaw and inevitable collision with the chosen dock.

The beauty of the PBR lay in its ability to beach easily on land, bow-on, with no damage to the propulsion system. An inherent drawback, however, was the fouling of the pumps, which could happen despite the grates installed over the pump inlets. Pump clogging could be terribly disconcerting and even dangerous. When traveling at high speed, a boat might unavoidably pass through a patch of river flotsam, suddenly lurch to the side of the clogged pump, and make an unwelcome U-turn known as a "flying 180." This was not necessarily dangerous, but could throw improperly stowed equipment and unprepared crew members completely out of the boat.

The river sailors lived, ate, fought, slept, and died in the boats. They traveled long miles in them, cooked in them, and nursed war wounds—their own and those of the Vietnamese—on the engine covers or in the limited spaces of the forward compartments.

*   *   *

I watched the Mekong treeline speed by and smiled as we continued the high speed run back from Dong Tam to the My Tho base. The thoughts of the PBR training, the old destroyer engine rooms and pumps, the days and endless nights standing watches on the bridges of ships at sea gave me a nostalgic twinge. The memory of the last night in San Francisco gave me another feeling which tugged at a familiar but lonely spot. I wiped the stubble on my face. I was tired from the long patrol, the strain of the firefight, and the feelings of remorse at having experienced my first casualty.

"Chief's waiting on the pier, Sir. You going to join us for breakfast?"

"Sure, I'd welcome the company." The river was beginning to feel a little like home—not really home, but kind of like a ship felt to her crew, a comforting and warm refuge.

Chapter III

The Journey

Lung

I awoke early to the sound of birds, buzzing flies, and mosquitos. Despite the visit by the armed Vietcong team, the night had passed without the sound of one explosion. Their return now seemed like a bad dream. My brothers still slept in their proper places. It was a good omen, a sign that today's trip on the river might be safe.

Remembering our planned journey to My Tho, I sprang off my straw mat and darted out the doorway to look at the sky. It was a clear light blue, streaked with orange from the rising sunlight. It would be a warm day, but I was seldom uncomfortable in the heat. The village of Phu Duc was usually cooled by a breeze from the main river, either from the northwest, upstream, or from the southeast, the direction of the open ocean, four hours by sampan down the Cua Tieu, past My Tho. A second main channel of the Mekong, called Cua Dai, flows to the south, discharging her vast waters into the sea near Kien Hoa, the thickly forested province forming the south bank.

I peered at my mother's mat and saw she was still asleep, a rare situation since the frail woman with prematurely gnarled hands was normally the first up, preparing an early meal of rice and fish cakes. Food, although plentiful in the delta, was precious, and its availability still demanded that the entire family participate in gathering. There was little money for us to buy food from the abundant markets. Instead we bartered with the fruit and vegetables we gathered ourselves to buy nuc mam, fish, chicken, pork, and tea from the market. It was not easy for a family with six children, but my brothers were adept at bringing home fish and crab from the river, a constant and reliable source of so many gifts.

Besides the fish and crab, the river provided water for the end-less fields of rice. Rice was the most important food and everyone had some association with the rice cycle. Some plowed with water buffalo, others planted, then replanted when the time was right and the fields were flooded. We all took part in the harvest. Some sifted the rice when dried, others hauled it in large bags, and we all ate rice daily. It was a measure of wealth and well-being of the peo-ple and a barometer of the times.

That day I was to prove I could go off to the big market in My Tho and sell the fruit I had packed carefully the day before in bas-kets lined with palm leaves and tied to the ends of a long pole. I would carry the smooth palm pole balanced on my shoulders or use it to help propel my brother's sampan down the narrow canal to meet the water taxi. We would return in the evening in the same boat before the night curfew began at dark.

I was excited and quickly woke my brother. I placed a metal tin of water on the charcoal stove and stirred and blew on the ash until the coals hidden at the bottom glowed brightly and rekindled the fire. Mother came in softly and began preparing a soup of rice, onions, and a few greens to warm us for the trip. Looking up from her work Mother asked, "Where will you meet Din?"

"At the water taxi, Mother. We'll be too busy to eat again until we get back. We'll save our money for the things we need here at home." My cousin Din, who came from a family of rice farmers in the next village, was equally frugal even though her family gener-ally had more money for things from the market. Nonetheless, the twelve-year-old Din also had to sell produce at the market.

The small room smelled of the ripe fruit stacked in the corner near the door. I hurried, anxious to be off and not to miss the water taxi. But I observed the family ritual, and the three of us quietly sipped hot soup and tea. I stood up, teased my brother along and told him to go out and bring the boat. I nodded to Mother, folded my hands, fingers extended in the traditional manner showing re-

spect, and backed out the door. Bending quickly, I picked up the
pole with its baskets loaded with mangos, bananas, and pineapple
and hurried to the canal. There in the early morning light I waited
for my brother.

I could see Cao approaching, poling his wooden sampan from its
resting place near the bank further down the canal. I smiled with
pride as the light transformed him into a splendid silhouette as he
effortlessly propelled the narrow boat alongside the dirt bank. "Get
in little sister," he sang in the musical tone he used to tease me. I
stepped in and deposited the two bundles on the boards in the center of the boat. I swung the palm pole into the water to assist Cao
in guiding the boat toward the main river and the island. As we
came around the first bend, I spotted a tightly-grouped knot of figures already waiting on the island.

Cao worked the sampan around to the outer side of the water
taxi, and I got ready to climb out. But first we paused to wait for
two water buffalo crossing the canal ahead of us. A young boy was
sitting on the back of the lead animal. We watched as the two giant
beasts of burden made their way across the canal and up the
muddy bank on the far side. The young boy rode with ease, swaying slightly with the motion of the buffalo as if joined to its back. I
had seen water buffalo as high as a man and as wide as five. They
were strong and never stalled in the mud or water of the flooded
rice paddies. The water buffalo, like the river, symbolized the solid
strength of farmers. The buffalo, brought to Vietnam by the Chinese centuries before, shared the strenuous work of the rice cycle
with the strong back of the rice farmer. The quantity of the animals, like the abundance of rice, was a barometer of the prosperity
of our land.

When the water buffalo had passed, Cao and I gathered our
poles and prepared to board the larger boat. We saw my cousin Din
already on the bank waiting for the water taxi. She waved as we approached. We picked her up in the sampan and Cao poled around

to the canal side of the water taxi, away from the throng. From the far side of the island the main channel of the Cua Tieu was not yet visible because of the heavy treeline which extended the length of the island like a spine, concealing the activity on the main river. As I pushed on the pole, keeping pace with my brother, the breeze from the main channel carried the sounds of the heavy boat engines. The roar of several deep-throated engines faded as the wind shifted. I paid no more attention as we watched the river and canal and smelled the charcoal of the early morning river life.

The crowd waited quietly. I stood in the sampan while my brother held us close alongside the larger boat with his pole. Din smiled. Excitement showed on her face. She was taller than I, but also thin and wiry. Her hair, like mine, hung long and straight to just below her shoulders, the sole sign of femininity which set us apart from the similarly clad young boys.

Suddenly, loud shooting began and the whole world changed. A sharp staccato of loud popping sounds erupted around us. We were engulfed in flying debris and what sounded like the buzzing of river insects. All our movements seemed deliberate and slow. The canopy of the water taxi disintegrated; chunks of wood flew into the air, and a jar of nuc mam burst, sending its contents into the air in a fine and fragrant spray. Everyone in the boat turned toward the treeline of the main river from where the sound came, horrified. I looked toward the sound and saw branches flying from the trees and tops of the grass severed from their stalks by steady streams of something heavy and hot pouring toward us from the river. I tried to warn Din, but the deafening sound drowned out my words.

People continued to board the boat quickly, throwing their bundles before them as they jumped and scrambled to safety. I placed one of my baskets on the rail of the taxi, and as I reached for the other, was suddenly struck by something heavy, which knocked my feet out from under me. The force of the blow hurled me into the air. I stared at the tree tops, the sun visible now high above the forest and village beyond. I felt suspended in mid-air as sky, water, trees, boats, and fruit whirled by in a dizzying chain. I felt the water spray engulf me as I seemed to drift higher, float, and then fall downward into a darkening hole.

I was suddenly in the bottom of my brother's boat. I had no feeling in either leg. I could not utter a sound, and just stared at Din. Her chest was an eruption of torn flesh; the material from her white blouse had turned red. I tried to reach out to Din to prevent her from falling, but I could not move. My brother grabbed Din to keep her from toppling into the water, and they fell together to the bottom of the sampan.

The sound of the shooting continued but seemed to move farther from the boats. I felt myself lifted again, this time by many hands. I floated toward the water taxi, under the cloth awning, away from the sun, and onto a wooden seat. I recognized the water taxi owner who was helping Din step into the large boat, blood running down the front of her smock. Din looked like a partially butchered animal and I became frightened for her. I could feel no pain, only an emptiness in both my legs. The water taxi started to move while several figures remained on the shore of the island, wailing in fear. I saw my brother poling furiously down the canal toward home as the water taxi chugged out from behind the treeline and into the main river channel of the Cua Tieu. I felt myself slip into a dark hole where the river should have been supporting me.

I stared at the river, afraid to close my eyes, and wondered why I had not been protected by the brown water as in the past. I emerged gradually from the darkness and did not know what was happening. "Where's Din, where's my fruit?" I muttered aloud. I tried to lift myself up to see what had happened to the packages we had packed so carefully with Mother's help. I must have lost them when I fell, or did Cao pick them up? For the first time in my life, I felt I could not control what was happening, and I did not like the feeling. I had always been in control, and now something had taken that command from me and left me like a piece of wood, adrift in the river to fall where I may. A feeling of total helplessness came over me.

I awoke and saw the end of the palm pole in the air with a piece of white cloth attached. I turned my head. At least I can move my head, I thought. I noticed the taxi owner was waving the pole frantically from inside the boat trying to attract the attention of someone mid-river. I managed with difficulty to turn my head the other way, and saw a fast moving boat coming toward us. It seemed to fly across the river like a water bug with a foaming white trail. I noticed a strange colored cloth flying from the top of the boat. I watched from where I lay, propped up on something soft, as the small boat approaching suddenly divided into two identical forms which continued to race toward us. As the two boats approached, I could make out the colors of red, white, and blue on the material. I assumed it was a flag. What a strange design!

The water taxi's engine stopped and the boat drifted slowly along the south bank, the green forest slipping past in slow motion. How beautiful, I thought. It was a view I had never seen before and for some reason it gave me strength.

The two green boats came closer and stopped a short distance away. One turned sideways abruptly as the second inched closer, the colored flag waving in the breeze. I noticed several men on the boat staring intently at our water taxi. They wore green clothes, round metal hats, shirts which looked heavy and too large for their bodies, and they carried guns. Most had strange light-skinned faces and wide, round eyes, but one was completely black with large white eyes. I had never seen such faces before. In a few moments, one of the boats was alongside ours and the owner was showing me to the strange-looking black man. A light-skinned man came closer, removed his metal hat, and peered down at me. He had golden short hair and blue eyes which, although strange, were soft and kind. He touched me somewhere I could not feel, turned, and said something I could not understand. His voice was loud, rough, and much lower than the voices of the Vietnamese men I knew. Another man appeared dressed the same, and helped lift me gently into their boat. They put me onto a flat board, and covered me with a prickly blanket. In a panic I thought of my cousin Din and tried to turn to look back inside the water taxi, but as soon as I did a large pale hand pushed my head firmly down onto the board. I heard voices in the same strange language and saw the golden haired man leaning over me talking and showing my feet to another man in green. I couldn't see my feet, but could clearly see the two men looking intently. The second man put his hand on my forehead for a moment, then drew the green blanket tightly around my chin. He spoke to the others, and seemed to tell them things first pointing into the distance, then to my feet. His words, spoken as if the chief, set the others in motion. He leaned over again and I noticed the man's eyes. They were a sort of blue-grey color and they were filled with water. I watched as the drops ran down his face. Odd, I thought. I had never seen Vietnamese men's eye's do that.

I lay back and thought of the events which had taken place during the past night and the morning, as the boat began to move quickly over the brown river water.

River Encounter

Peter

Our two-boat patrol was completing an all night curfew-enforcement watch on the upper Cua Tieu. It was late April in 1967, shortly after the first grey light cracked over the disappearing darkness. With a mouth tasting of stale metallic garlic, I craved the strong, hot navy coffee waiting back at the My Tho base camp, still an hour away downriver. I noticed the captain on the second boat in the patrol waving and pointing into the distance. His boat was fifty yards astern our lead PBR. I followed his gestures and saw a fully-loaded Vietnamese water taxi about eighty feet long enter the main river from a canal where several heavily-armored and slow-moving monitors from the U.S. riverine forces had been shooting. A long pole with a piece of white cloth on the top was waving from the taxi. The riverine force monitors in mid-river stopped firing briefly and I directed our two-boat patrol cautiously toward the water taxi. I ordered a further reduction in speed. "Keep her covered," I yelled. We were always careful with this type of encounter. In the past, several of our PBRs had been ambushed and seriously damaged by Vietcong B-40 rockets in similar situations.

We let the water taxi approach us. The improving light allowed us to see the damage done to the craft. Our engines idled as I motioned the bullet-riddled water taxi to approach our position as we maneuvered the boats as far as possible from the riverbank. "Play it exactly by the book," I said slowly into the radio mike. The river patrols had an automatic procedure for this type of scenario. One boat stood off covering the first, which then ordered the Vietnamese boat alongside. With all crew members holding weapons at the ready, we could back off and destroy a sampan quickly if it opened fire.

"Looks like more than fifty people aboard, it's not likely a booby trap," I said into the mike. Two answering clicks from the cover boat came over the speaker, acknowledging my comments. Our boat provided cover while the second PBR took the taxi alongside.

Petty Officer Roderick Davis, captain of the second boat, was one of the most mature and seasoned sailors in his section. He was on his second voluntary year in Vietnam, and loved working with the Vietnamese. Davis was good with the language, speaking Vietnamese better than any of the other men. I preferred Davis as the boat captain in the cover boat on my patrols. As river section operations officer in My Tho, I rotated my duties to monitor the performance of all ten of the sections' boat crews, but I still preferred to work with Davis when the mission was delicate or dangerous.

As the taxi reached the open water, I caught sight of a line of smoke visible from upstream in mid-river. More smoke burst in puffs as the delayed sound arrived—a continuous staccato of gunfire. I could distinguish the high-pitched sound of small arms fire and the lower, slower pop of larger caliber guns. Our attention now riveted upriver, we watched the blue smoke of diesel engines billow over the water and made out the dark green outline of strange flat-looking boats that appeared half submerged. A line of white waves pushed out in front of the boats as they moved slowly away from the water taxi and continued upriver. I could still see the spurts of orange flame and gold and red tracers coming from the boats. The slowly moving green figures looked like dark monsters moving against the current, still firing aimlessly into the treeline. Debris flew as their rounds hit the shore. Every few seconds I could see a line of tracers arch high into the sky and disappear in the sunlight.

As our boat stood off waiting, I watched Davis climb aboard the water taxi. After a few minutes he reappeared, carrying a small figure and followed by a Vietnamese man. Davis boarded his PBR, then called me on the radio, "We've got two wounded Viets, Boss. Two little girls, one hit bad. Advise. Over."

The three crafts were drifting about a hundred yards from the river's south bank, not far from the spot where the water taxi had first emerged from the canal. The heavy riverine boats were in a column to the north about 500 meters away. Through my field glasses I could just make out an officer atop a monitor turret watching our patrol with his own binoculars. I decided to take the wounded and move away from the scene as fast as possible. I had a terrible feeling that the two casualties might be the result of weapons testing from the heavy riverine units.

I watched as the second wounded figure was taken aboard Davis' boat, obviously another child. Davis signalled, "All secure Boss."

"Okay Davis, cast off from the taxi," I started to respond when a loud boom and a splash exploded near the cover boat. Both boats sprang into motion and wheeled together in a wide arc away from the water taxi and from the south bank of the river. Several small arms shots cracked in our direction and a second rocket, with its tell-tale plume of black smoke, arched from the riverbank toward Davis' boat. It passed well overhead and detonated in the water between the two boats. I yelled to the forward 50-caliber machine gunner, who put in a short burst in the direction of the rocket. "Pin the bastard down 'til we're clear," I shouted as the spray from another near-miss poured over the boat.

Lung

I awoke and watched the events as if detached. The pale Americans moved differently but seemed kind. I watched, unable to move.

The sound of a different kind of gun began popping while I watched in terror from a flat wooden board. I peered at the men in green as they began moving with quick, jerky actions. They had put on their round metal hats again and I heard the boat roar like a lion. I watched the brown water turn to white spray as we leapt forward. We seemed to fly away, with the men frozen like statues, all looking at the same point on the riverbank. Suddenly the water next to the boat erupted in a huge splash, and the boat swung wildly in the air. One man pointed to the trees on the left canal bank and shouted something. The boat again surged forward and swerved into a turn. The big guns on the front began a long chatter while shiny hot metal tubes rained over the boat. I heard a *swoosh* as a black object passed overhead, trailing dark smoke. It disappeared and was followed by a loud *wump*. A shower of water poured over the whole craft. The engines continued running with a high speed whine and again I heard popping sounds, this time from a different direction and farther away. One man shouted into a radio and made a pumping gesture with his arm over his head so the other boat could see. A sharp *ping* followed and I watched as the strange pale man was showered with green paint chips flying off the metal plating next to his body. He covered his face then began the motion again, somehow unhurt. As he turned his head to avoid the spray of chips, his eyes briefly met mine and he gave me a silly grin, then turned back to the radio. I thought, how strange and childish these men are!

The boat kept moving at high speed. I heard a moan somewhere near me, and with great difficulty turned and noticed Din sitting on the board across from me. A large white sheet was tied around her chest. There was no sign of blood. "Din," I cried and blinked to clear my eyes of the river water running down my face. I wanted to hug my cousin but could not raise my arms. I felt a wave of relief to see Din looked fine except for the white wrapping. Her eyes were bright and full of excitement. She even smiled when she saw me looking at her.

I noticed that the boat had come to a halt alongside a second identical craft. Someone was doing something to my legs. I could feel the movement and pressure but no pain. The boat started to move again, more slowly than before, and continued for a long time. I tried to sleep but could not. I could only think of my brother, the fruit I had lost, and how I would tell Mother what had happened.

Peter

The two boats, now in a close column about fifty yards apart, ran a racetrack course. "Hold fire until I say," I instructed. The line of sight was directly into the island located just to the river side of the village Phu Duc. Roderick Davis knew the site well, and recognized the Vietcong tactic of enticing the PBRs to return fire into inhabited areas, worsening the situation by causing additional casualties to civilians—unmistakably the work of Americans.

"Shit . . . Sir," muttered the forward gunner on the lead boat. "The bastards did it again."

"Check fire," I repeated on the radio hand-set to Davis' boat. "Need to get out of here," I yelled. "Too much sampan traffic." We could see other small boats full of market-bound civilians now piling up at the mouth of the canal, all destined for the My Tho market. Again I spoke into the mike. This time I reported the exchange of fire to the local army sector in the rudimentary three-letter code we shared with the local U.S. advisors in the Ben Tre area.

My PBR pulled alongside the other so I could check the casualties. As we drew together and the water taxi faded away toward the canal, I saw a young girl lying on the engine cover. Her left foot was barely attached to the lower leg by sinews. A pool of blood was spreading on the engine cover as Davis and another crew member worked on a battle dressing for the girl. I stepped into the second boat and looked down. The young girl's eyes were open; she was fully awake and staring at me. She did not utter a sound.

Growing angry at the situation, I dispatched Davis. "Don't spare the horses Davis. Take them back to My Tho province hospital at flank speed."

"Aye, Boss," Davis responded. I jumped the gunnel back into the boat and turned it toward the dark green riverine craft in the distance. The cover boat sped off trailing a white rooster tail of river water. Davis' large form masked the two tiny Vietnamese figures huddled on the engine covers. It was a forty-minute run at top speed downstream to our base at My Tho.

The smell of nuc mam fish sauce hung in the air just as it seemed to do around the locals. The betel nut and nuc mam odors clung to our clothing and permeated everything we wore. Yet the Vietnamese said we Americans smelled strongly—a different smell caused by a diet consisting of more meat than theirs. As a result, we chewed garlic cloves at the urging of the river police riding our patrols. They claimed our strong body odors gave us away well before the sounds of the boats could be heard.

Oh, the tastes and smells of that war! Our memories might fade, but whenever I smell charcoal smoke, fish sauce, and garlic, the images of the river come to life with remarkable intensity. The quiet babble of women's voices, cackling as they did when we searched the endless sampans on the brown river, take me back to those scenes. Women crowded in tiny huts balanced on minuscule floating wooden hulls, the aroma of betel nut in the air, sweet and pungent, musty but clean. It is a smell unknown in the West, but to me it is reminiscent of fear, suffering, and sorrow.

Ours was an isolated, grim world of struggle on the river, consisting of the PBR base in My Tho, the American army advisors, the Seventh ARVN Division, the Giang Khan river police, the Vietcong, and the civilians caught in the middle. "What a mess," I mumbled, as I thought of how the other PBR sailors shared the drama of the conflict with each of the other organizations. I looked ahead as we closed on large green monitors. We were intimidated by the arrival of the massive American navy units on our river. Hundreds of all-U.S. units like the riverine forces were pouring into the war, operating without the expertise and compassion developed by those who had spent long months working with the other players in the contest on the lower Mekong. New American units regarded the local Vietnamese regular army and local paramilitary forces as untrustworthy and American commanders sought to operate with total operational secrecy due to the Vietcong's infiltration of nearly all local military formations. Successful operational autonomy, however, was impossible to achieve.

Our single PBR approached the lead monitor and the crew prepared to tie up alongside, still gathering the empty cartridge casings which littered the decks and clattered noisily. I jumped aboard the slow-moving monitor and approached the young navy lieutenant I had seen sitting high in a perch on the turret of the heavily-armored vessel.

"Hey Lieutenant, you need assistance?" I called out over the engine noise. There was no answer. The lieutenant just stared back in embarrassed silence. "Why the hell are you firing into that area?" I asked again, pointing to the treeline. No more hostile fire had come from the shore since the short burst aimed at our PBRs when we ·

picked up the wounded Vietnamese from the water taxi. The pink-faced lieutenant pointed downriver.

"We're cleared to test-fire weapons here. Don't need any help, thanks."

"Did you see the locals in there, hundreds of them and a market and water taxis?" I shouted over the staccato of a 20-millimeter cannon, which had commenced fire into the treeline.

"Tough shit," answered the lieutenant. "It's a free-fire zone. We've got clearance from the CTU (Commander Task Unit) to fire in there." He pointed down the main river channel, referring to the large, floating barracks ship, the USS *Benewah* (APB 35). In recent weeks she had been riding at anchor in mid-river near the U.S. Ninth Infantry Division base at Dong Tam, about ten miles west of our PBR base area. The *Benewah* was the flagship for the Riverine Force commander. I stared into the lieutenant's face. The young officer looked back blankly, then shrugged. "Can't help it buddy, war is hell. What're you guys anyway, fuckin' slope lovers?" I stared in disbelief and fought the urge to shoot the young man out of his perch with my Colt 45. I shook my head in disgust and turned back to the PBR. We cast off, and headed our boat downriver for the run back to home base.

Chapter IV

River Adventures

Peter

After returning to the boat basin in My Tho, I met Leading Chief Smith, the senior chief bo'sun who doubled as the command senior enlisted advisor, morale and welfare officer, and did a bit of everything else to help run the one-hundred man river patrol unit.

I drained a cup of strong navy coffee shortly after we landed. "Chief, where did Davis take the wounded Viets?"

"Province Hospital, Sir. He'd like you to come over there right away, to see what happened to the two girls."

We jumped in the section's jeep and left the pier area, turning into the crowded My Tho Boulevard and weaving through the thick crowd. My Tho was a beautiful town, with a wide thoroughfare running north to south, ending in a shabby but attractive park on the riverbank. To the south of town flowed the Cua Tieu, a wide expanse of swift brown water nearly a mile across. The sea wall was crowded with sampans, water taxis, and boats of every description. To the west on the upriver bank stood a smart-looking building with a red tile roof, beautifully shuttered windows, and an open patio squatting on stilts over the water.

The building had been a yacht club during the pre-war French days, the Japanese navy's river headquarters during the war, and was now the headquarters of the My Tho South Vietnamese river forces. There were several American navy advisors assigned to the Vietnamese river command who were seldom seen in town. They spent their time out on the river in their old French river boats, escorting the supply convoys in the canals to and from Saigon. The South Vietnamese unit had armored monitors and landing craft dating from the French war in the late 1940s and 1950s which were

not as well-equipped or armored as the new American mobile
riverine craft.

"Chief, seems like there's no war going on in My Tho. Look," I
pointed ahead where two beautiful young Vietnamese women were
riding bicycles in brilliant white silk au-dais. The ends of the flowing skirts were tucked neatly under their seats to keep them from
the spokes. They giggled as they wove in and out of the morning
traffic. They could have been on any main boulevard in the world,
far from the war and suffering that was here in their backyard.

"Yeah, Lieutenant," the chief drawled in his thick Alabama accent. "Makes me wonder sometimes what the hell we're doin' here.
If these people don't know they're at war, maybe we shouldn't remind them."

"Look out!" The jeep swerved as two dust-covered, two-and-one-
half-ton army trucks ran through the intersection without stopping,
causing the cyclists to scatter like frightened chickens.

"Son of a bitch. They don't even slow down," the chief roared as
he pulled the jeep off the side of the road and reentered the main
stream of traffic which flowed on as if nothing had happened.

"Looks like we're never too far from the reminders. Just when
you forget about the war and start enjoying the place, you get
jerked back to reality, like this morning on the river. It was one of
the most beautiful sunrises I've ever seen."

"Yes Sir, only you can't enjoy it much when some son of a bitch is
trying to pop your ass off from the riverbank. War is hell, Sir."

I recoiled at the words. "Don't say that, Chief." I was thinking of
the pink-faced navy lieutenant sitting atop his armored command
monitor, firing with abandon at nothing in particular. He had used
those same words. "I've heard that phrase once too often."

"Sorry, Sir." The chief glanced at me suspiciously as he maneuvered the jeep through the crowds. We arrived at the hospital and
wearing our black berets, entered the main hall of the sprawling

building. The Province Hospital, built in the French days, had once been an elegant structure boasting the lines of colonial French architecture. It consisted of a cluster of two-story buildings connected by red tile-covered breezeways with arches and columns. Although badly in need of fresh paint, it still looked graceful. We were met by a tall, slender Vietnamese nurse dressed in a long white au-dai. A brilliant white cap bearing a delicate red cross was perched on shiny black hair rolled high in a French bun. She bowed slightly. "Gentlemen, are you looking for Mr. Davis?"

This dainty woman speaking perfect English seemed out of place in the dusty town, teeming with mud-splattered military vehicles and war equipment. Vietnam was full of contrasts. Beauty shared the stage with ugliness: the relics of bitter conflict and anguish appeared alongside of elegance and charm. The angelic figure of the nurse glided over the red tile floor, silk au-dai fluttering as she led us to another wing of the hospital. The building smelled of a mixture of antiseptic, betel nut, and charcoal smoke. It was clean, but crowded with the debris of human misery swept up from the struggle on the river and the intertwining waterways and rice fields.

We entered a room containing twelve cots, each occupied by a small body. Large black eyes peered at our coarse green uniforms. The children lay in odd postures forced by the unnatural constrictions of wounds, broken limbs, and bandages too large for small bodies. The young patients who were awake stared, not missing a single movement of the visitors. Despite their discomfort, not one child made a sound. These are the children of the Mekong, I thought as we walked by the tiny figures. These children would suffer quietly through the current turmoil, and later slip into the postwar exodus of the "boat people," always agonizing silently and without tears.

"Your friends are in here." The nurse motioned toward a nearby bed. First-Class Signalman Roderick Davis sat on a low stool by an end cot in his sweat-stained fatigues. His short sun-bleached hair lay matted against his forehead and he held his black beret in his hands.

"Good morning, Dai Ui." An unexpected but familiar voice came from across the room. Co Thuong, the American navy's official interpreter, sat perched on a chair on the other side of the bed, wearing a colorful au-dai. Her face bore the more flattened features of Chinese heritage. "Surprised to see me here already?"

Co Thuong, called the "Dragon Lady" by the sailors, somehow managed to be present at every major navy event in town in order to help with the language. In the heat of the hospital room, little translation was necessary to relay the thoughts and feelings of the small group standing around the bed. The Americans stared in discomfort, equating the scene with imagined parallels back home in America.

"She's okay, Boss," Roderick whispered, breaking the silence. "Her name's Lung. Means 'short one.'" He smiled, embarrassed at his immersion in the situation. From the beginning it was obvious that the young girl would lose the foot that had been dangling from severed tendons. She had not cried or made the slightest sound as the boat had raced for the My Tho landing.

"I called ahead by radio to have a jeep waiting to bring us here," Roderick explained. It was a short trip across town to the hospital, located in a quiet section of town several blocks from the busy province headquarters. The staff of American, Australian, and Filipino volunteer doctors and nurses had been helpful and understanding, and admitted the injured child immediately.

"The doctor said we made it just in time. I guess the shock was gettin' to her. But we kept her from losing too much blood." Roderick's eyes showed the combined fatigue of the night on patrol, the tension of the early morning firefight, and now the release of anxiety in the hospital. "Doc said it wouldn't have mattered if we'd got here sooner, the foot was . . . well, it was too far gone anyway. We couldn't do much else, it just. . . ."

I put my hand on the young sailor's shoulder. "You did everything right, Davis. Don't worry, it couldn't be helped."

"Yeah Boss, but it shouldn't 've happened. It was probably those new riverine units. They don't know the goddamn area, they don't know their ass . . . it could'a been the VC too, trying to make us and the riverines shoot in there. Who knows? God, we tried. . . ." I shook him gently as he fought to keep control. "Don't sweat it Roderick. There's nothing more we can do."

I looked down at the small form in the cot. The uneven length of the limbs showing under the white sheet made it clear Lung had lost the leg a few inches below the knee. "I've been here with her since the amputation, but she just starting coming to before you came in." Apparently asleep when we entered, the young girl suddenly opened her eyes and focused on us. She showed no emotion and did not cry, but her first smile made us choke with feeling. "Look Sir," Davis whispered. "She's awake now."

Lung's eyes shifted around to each of us and, while still smiling, she tried to scan the room. "Din?" She whispered, looking for her cousin.

Roderick rattled off something in Vietnamese that I could not understand. "She was treated and released. Her chest wounds weren't bad enough to keep her here," Davis translated.

We stared at the small face and the surprising smile. To us she represented the essence of the children of Vietnam who were always present, yet never subdued by the suffering and chaos. They possessed a tenacity and resilience which was difficult to defeat. It became clear years later what masterful survivors the young Vietnamese really were, and what marvelous gifts of drive and initiative they mysteriously brought with them.

*   *   *

The sailors' participation in the healing process of the tiny Lung became one tangible aspect of the war which they could visibly influence. On their own initiative, sailors from the river unit visited Lung every day, bringing her small gifts to brighten up her hospital room. Odd bits of American life appeared at her bedside, simple trinkets the sailors either possessed already, or received in packages from home. A small Statue of Liberty stood on her bed stand. A pin reading "I Love the Big Apple" showing a big red heart was affixed to her pillow. Boxes of badly crushed chocolate-chip cookies and fudge were constantly at hand. We made sure that she had extra food, and with the help of the Dragon Lady, Co Thuong, we coaxed the doctors and nurses to give her special treatment.

Lung soon became our mascot and the most celebrated patient in the hospital. A routine developed, with sailors returning from long patrols on the river stopping by the hospital to see Lung. They dropped off small packets of crackers and chewing gum from the combat rations opened on patrol. Eventually she grew stronger, and her little stump healed sufficiently for her to hobble around the hospital. The sailors fabricated a pair of crude crutches with the help of old Mr. Phu, the handyman at the army compound and a legend in the area.

After her discharge, Lung disappeared with some visiting villagers. A week after she left the hospital however, she mysteriously appeared outside the Victory Hotel navy compound on her crutches. Co Thuong, who was by this time as much a part of Lung's life as the sailors were, found her hovering near the gate afraid to try to enter past the guards, barbed-wire, and surrounding sand bags. Co Thuong recognized her and brought her in.

"Look who I found, gentlemen." Thuong opened the door and led the young Lung into the room. When she entered the river section office, she stared with apprehension at the surroundings: maps, rosters, weapons, and boat gear cluttered the room. The prevailing colors of olive-drab and khaki gave the room a gloomy character. When she suddenly spotted Roderick Davis her face brightened and burst into a smile. "Trung Shi," she said softly—the Vietnamese for sergeant.

Davis was embarrassed by her attention. "Thank you," he murmured.

The sailors cleared a small area at a desk for Lung, and she became a regular fixture over the next few months. She helped tidy up and did odd jobs to keep busy and out of the way. She brought water and coffee during the pre-patrol briefings, and helped pack the daily rations into the patrol containers for transport to the boat basin. She filled the water coolers with ice, and cleaned them after the patrols. Roderick and Co Thuong took her to the My Tho market and bought her a new set of clothes, including her first silk au-dai, worn by young girls for the first time at age ten.

Since Lung was unable to return to the Ben Tre Province where she had lived, the PBR unit unofficially adopted her. Ben Tre was a Vietcong-controlled province and an area the navy avoided. A neighboring river section had recently lost three crewmen, including the section commander, Lieutenant Donn Witt, to Vietcong recoilless rifle fire from heavily-bunkered canals near the capital of Ben Tre. Earlier attempts to return Lung to her home village of Phu Duc failed when the district chief warned that there would be serious repercussions and hardships on the family and their fellow villagers because of Lung's relationship with the Americans. The story of her rescue and convalescence had traveled via the far-reaching Vietnamese grapevine and was widely known. The true details of her rescue, however, did not fit Vietcong propaganda, which painted Americans as cruel and uncaring foreign occupiers.

Several weeks after Lung's release from the hospital, our patrols found propaganda posters hanging in trees along the river and canals showing a picture of Lung on crutches. The text stated that American imperialists had wounded and then kidnapped the young girl from Ben Tre Province. Similar leaflets were found floating around the markets along the river in Dinh Tuong, Ben Tre, and Binh Dai provinces. In a move to counter the propaganda, we often took Lung with us on patrols called MEDCAPS (Medical Civic Action Patrols). These excursions carried a volunteer doctor and nurse into remote contested villages to hold public medical calls and distribute medical supplies and school materials in an effort to bolster the local South Vietnamese government's image. Such visits drew large crowds, primarily made up of elderly men and women and children badly in need of basic medicines. The MEDCAPS were usually three-boat PBR patrols embarking a squad of regional or provincial infantry (Rf/Pf), to provide a cordon of adequate ground security. We took Lung along on many of these MEDCAPS to show the locals that she was well cared for. Lung was also a living example of a successful medical evacuation by our PBRs. The lesson was not lost on the local delta inhabitants, and soon we experienced an increase in numbers of seriously wounded and sick Vietnamese hailing our patrols for emergency evacuation.

Nevertheless, it proved best to keep Lung in My Tho, with the family contact maintained through her cousin Din, whose family had relocated near the river market. In this way Lung was in the relative safety of the town of My Tho, and her presence would not deepen the split loyalties so much a part of life in the delta.

Every Thursday evening Lieutenant Lowell Webb, Roderick, and I would take Lung to the army compound for broiled steaks, the one luxury we enjoyed until the Tet Offensive. Mr. Phu, who was the coordinator of the domestic help in the U.S. Army advisors' compound, sat with us on those warm evenings and entertained Lung by translating the American folk stories we narrated to him. In turn, Phu would tell us Vietnamese children's stories, to the delight of Lung. Phu, like the Dragon Lady, became a key figure in Lung's life with the Americans.

Roderick adjusted Lung's crutches to fit, and made them more comfortable by adding thick foam pads to the tops. With Co Thuong's help, we found a Catholic boarding school for girls and enrolled Lung for the next school year, while the river unit organized a monthly collection for the small tuition. We discovered she had never attended school, although already ten years old. Her entire life had been spent in the village, gathering vegetables, fuel, and fruit to sell at the market.

School was new to Lung and at first difficult. It was hard to get her to remain at the school rather than visit with the sailors in the navy compound. Eventually, with Co Thuong's patience and guidance, she grew fond of the Catholic sisters and liked her studies. Every navy pay-day a cigar box appeared in the section orderly's office marked "for Em Lung." It was always stuffed full of dollars by the end of the day. Davis bought her several more high-collared silk au-dais in the special light pastel colors required by the school. Roderick and I applied to the World Rehabilitation Fund for an artificial leg to be made in their Saigon center.

Lung often accompanied us when we visited nearby villages as part of the support plan offered to the more remote villages close to the river or canals. These were prime locations for the American river patrol to offer defensive support. Many of the liaison visits became elaborate displays of hospitality by the host village leaders, who sought to show their gratitude for the valuable assistance we provided from the river. The river was, after all, the lifeline of the villages and their economic tie with the rest of the world and it was imperative that they retain free use of the river and canals. Thus the American river forces were welcomed with open arms. Lung's presence with the American boats served as a symbol of good intentions, and she was warmly received by the local village elders. In this way, the river units made many fast friends along the reaches of the upper Mekong from Vinh Long south along the Cua Tieu and the lower branch, called the Cua Dai.

One of the favorite villages was called Ap Phu Dinh, located off the main river in Binh Dai Province. During the first visit with Lung accompanying, our meeting with the village chief and senior U.S. army advisor was followed by a festive lunch at the district chief's home. We found a large table set with a typical Vietnamese spread consisting of numerous plates laden with chicken, pork, beef,

bowls of different vegetables, and small saucers filled with nuc
mam, in which floated thinly chopped red peppers and garlic. The
rice stood in a large tin pan, glistening in a way that only the Vietnamese can achieve. On the table were bottles of Ba Mui Ba (33)
beer from the famous brewery of the French days, a colorful fruit
juice, and a single bottle of Johnny Walker Red. Thieu Ta (Major)
Linh, the district chief and host, was beaming. Like most Vietnamese, he loved to please the foreign allies by providing the very
best available. It was an impressive feast, but not unusual for a gra-
cious Vietnamese host. An older lady, apparently Linh's mother,
worked quickly and quietly refilling the plates, smiled at the Americans and watched them eat. Linh's wife and three young girls sat
apart from the table and watched the proceedings.

"We welcome you, our allies." Linh toasted. "We also welcome
one of our daughters of the river we have heard you have taken in
as part of your family." The district chief was one of the most popular in the area and loved to celebrate in the mixed company of
American navymen and local U.S. army advisors. "Let this union by
a young Vietnamese girl with the Americans be a symbol of our co-
operation and joint effort," the major continued in his good English. "We appreciate your support in these difficult times, and that
you voluntarily share in the common dangers on the river. Let us all
join in a toast to the speedy end to the conflict and a peaceful return to your homes." He raised his glass and looked at us sitting in
our sweat-stained, jungle fatigue uniforms. He then glanced at the
thin figure of Lung, standing between the large and ungainly figures
of two oversized Americans.

It was a pity that the media rarely saw scenes such as this, with
the people of both sides united in common concern, free from the
apprehension and distrust which usually surrounded the presence
of the all-American troop units. The media focus in Vietnam was in-
creasingly on the carnage and mass destruction wrought by the use

of American firepower against an elusive foe, and it was this elu-
siveness that helped cause the tremendous use of force to become
misdirected against the harmless and struggling masses of Southeast Asia.

The lunch continued as we devoured most of the food, a welcome break from our normal diet of C-rations and canned Spam.
Lung became a part of the party and was treated by the host as a
special symbol of our successful relationship. The relaxed scene
came to an end as we returned to our heavily armed boats, and said
good-bye to our hosts. Both sides charged their weapons and
girded for the night—still owned by the Vietcong.

For those Americans who worked as advisors or in small units
with close daily contact with the Vietnamese, the war became a
personal involvement. This was not the case for larger U.S. units,
which arrived en mass, lived in large U.S. compounds, and inter-
acted with the local populace only when on operations. I understood how the war could take on a totally different face given the
two types of experiences. With each day in the delta, we learned
more about Vietnamese life, and often these insights shed new
light on the deeper aspects of the conflict.

In late summer of 1967, I was called in to see the Binh Dai
Province chief to coordinate operations to apprehend Vietcong tax
collectors. "We must take harsh measures to prevent the VC from
imposing their own de facto rule," insisted the province chief, a
Vietnamese lieutenant colonel who was held in great esteem by his
people. "These tax collectors must be eliminated at all costs." At
the time I did not grasp the full impact the VC tax collectors had on
the province chief's authority, but I soon found out.

In response to the urging of the Binh Dai Province chief, we set
up an operation plan for use on the lower Cua Dai River, which
bordered on his province. The plan called for encouraging the river
populace to inform South Vietnamese forces, or in the case of

boats enroute to market, one of our PBR patrols, as soon as they encountered VC attempts to collect taxes. The plan worked to a degree. Disgruntled farmers, forced at gun point to part with hardearned rice and other products, often came to us. We in turn attempted to arrange ambushes or patrols where the tax collectors were operating. In one case, I intercepted a disgruntled farmer whose entire rice load was confiscated when he refused to pay a tax. He was so angry he offered to direct a night patrol to intercept and capture the culprits. Wary of ambush, but keen to exploit the opportunity, I met the angry farmer in a small town on the river near the province capital. With a reinforced three-boat patrol, I took a squad of regional force troops—just enough to extend our capabilities ashore if needed, but not enough to impair our speed and maneuverability.

We picked up our small infantry squad and the informer before midnight on a moonless night ten miles south of Binh Dai. I put the informer in my lead boat with the English-speaking river policeman, Sergeant Dinh. The frightened informer indicated we should head south toward the estuary where the tax collecting team would be hiding in a large ocean-going junk anchored in a cove near the open South China Sea. With some trepidation I followed his directions until we were bouncing along in seas higher than we normally saw in the protected waters of the upper rivers. Being in the open sea gave me some comfort, since it was highly unlikely we would be surprised by concealed Vietcong, who fought mostly from treelines. The further we were from land, the more the advantage shifted to our patrol.

Finally, after running several hours at full power, the informer pointed to a cluster of dim lights bobbing on the horizon. We slowly made our way toward them, running cautiously upwind to the anchored nest. It was totally dark: the only other lights visible were a few flickering lights marking the eastern shoreline of Binh Dai. As we drew nearer to the nest of moored junks, the informer became more and more nervous. Sergeant Dinh took the precaution of holding a pistol on him, and told him that if we were ambushed he would immediately be shot. We approached the lights, which appeared to come from three large junks tied to a cluster of fish stakes. As planned, two of our boats remained downwind about fifty yards, while my lead boat drifted in on one engine—with crew and Rf troops with blackened faces ready to spring.

There was no sign of life aboard the junks as we approached; it was 3:15 A.M. The night sea air was cool and the swell and light wind made sufficient background noise to muffle any sound we made. At first I planned to board carrying an M-16 with Dinh and the Rfs, but a glance at the pitching junks changed my mind. I left the M-16 and drew my regulation .45 automatic, chambered a round and then, still feeling naked, I took a kay-bar knife and put it in my belt. We made the side and jumped aboard. Dinh and three Rf troopers bounded below and reappeared on deck with two sleepy looking Vietnamese in black pajamas. We quickly searched the other two junks and found two more men and a huge cache of paper Vietnamese piasters, hundreds of thousands, tied in bundles and wrapped in plastic. Three Chinese 9-mm pistols were found hidden in the bilges. With only four men aboard the three junks, it was apparent the full team was not present. Dinh returned to the junk with the informer, who immediately lunged at the oldest prisoner with a bamboo boat hook he scooped up off deck. Dinh managed to subdue him before he did any permanent damage. We loaded the money and the four bound captives into the lead PBR. Concerned that the others might return, and certain we would never see them in the pitch dark, we prepared to shove off. Suddenly, a red-lensed searchlight from one of the cover boats cut through the darkness and illuminated a large sampan approaching from upwind. There were at least four figures aboard. A brief melee followed while dark figures and cargo splashed into the water and green tracer rounds burst wildly from the sampan. The light remained on for merely a second, but it triggered an impressive display of fireworks.

The two waiting PBRs had been alert, had heard the engine approaching, and waited until the last moment before ilumminating the sampan. I had banned the use of radios to preclude compromise of our positions. I was still aboard the junk nest when the shooting started. After the first rounds of green tracer began to arc from the sampan—unmistakably AK-47 fire—the large craft was at once laced with red tracer fire from six PBR 50-caliber machine guns. The target was immediately shredded into glowing fragments.

The firing from the sampan ended as abruptly as it began, and the cover boats moved in and began sifting through the wreckage in the water. I jumped back aboard the lead boat and shoved off with our cargo of four frightened men and the stash of Vietnamese currency. One badly wounded young man was recovered from the water along with three more bundles of cash and two badly mangled bodies, one apparently a woman. We could not find the fourth person. We left the scene and made our way back into the Cua Dai estuary.

As we steamed at flank speed, our four bound prisoners distributed in two of the PBRs, I made the serious navigational error of underestimating the larger tides on the lower river estuary. While leading the two cover boats in column at more than 25 knots, my boat suddenly struck a muddy river bar. The shock of grounding at that speed was so great the rear gunner and the two VC prisoners were catapulted over the side into the river, while engine covers, amunition cans, grenades, and weapons flew forward in a cascade of confusion. Luckily the mud was deep, and while we were seriously aground in several inches of water with both jacuzzi pumps clogged, the hull was not damaged. We recovered our prisoners, who were hand cuffed together, and the gunner, all totally covered with mud. The two cover boats astern had quickly sheared to either side of the lead boat and remained safely in deeper water.

Happily, the tide was coming in but the sun was also rising. There I sat with my victorious command, high and dry, not one hundred yards from the nearest treeline, silhouetted by the rising sun, waiting for the tide to put enough water under the hull to continue home. To our southeast lay the vast Vietcong-controlled area of lower Binh Dai.

In the early hours of the pre-dawn we charged our weapons, tied the prisoners to the after machine gun stanchion, and hunkered down to await the tide. It was an eerie feeling: our defenses of speed and maneuverability gone, stuck in the mud within small arms range of the riverbank, exposed to every danger. We sat nervously scouring the high elephant grass on the riverbank for the tell-tale muzzle flash of a B-40 rocket, or worse, a recoilless rifle. The only sound was the river water lapping the hull and the buzz of insects. I called the My Tho operations center and ordered two standby PBRs to begin the two-hour run downriver toward us for refueling, and requested the navy Seawolf helicopter gunships be placed on standby in case we were hit. Each minute passed in painful agony as the light increased and the tide inched higher. Finally, the sun cracked over the South China Sea in a huge orange ball. We floated free and continued back to province headquarters at Binh Dai.

In the province chief's exuberance over our catch, which turned out to be a major cell of the Vietcong tax collecting organization in his area, the Vietnamese lieutenant colonel pulled me aside and offered me a reward for our victory. "I'll give you one-third of all the taxes you and your crews collect from now on in my name." And he handed me a note printed in Vietnamese and English stating that each Vietnamese boat over five meters in length stopped on the river by a PBR was to pay the amount of 20 piasters; boats over ten meters would pay 40 piasters. The paper was authorization for me and my PBR sailors to levy a tax on all the river boats we stopped and searched. The province chief would then receive the remaining seventy percent of all we collected. This was an award based on his legal authority as province chief to collect taxes.

At first I was astounded, but eventually understood. It was an age-old custom for the leaders in Vietnam to exact tolls or tariffs from all under their charge as a normal matter due to their position. The colonel thought nothing was more legitimate than to use his taxing authority to recognize the usefulness of the American PBR force and to repay us in kind for the advantages we commanded on the rivers. It was not considered corruption, merely the traditional Vietnamese way.

After turning the offer down politely, I pondered the matter. It was indicative of the dichotomy in our thinking. Some senior U.S. politicians, who were opposed to all aspects of the American involvement in Vietnam, had seized the issue of corruption in the South Vietnamese government as a key rationale for ending our assistance. But once on the scene, we knew that to attempt to reform the culture and traditional behavior in Southeast Asia to democratic American standards was certainly beyond our capability.

Word finally arrived from the World Rehabilitation Center that Lung's artificial leg was ready for fitting. Roderick and I decided to take Lung to Saigon by jeep. It was a Friday morning and it was theoretically prohibited for Americans to drive to or from Saigon. Ground transport to the capital was restricted to Thursdays in the weekly convoy which traveled with helo gunship, armor, and armed jeep escort. Too many individual American travelers had been ambushed on the two-hour drive down Highway 4. But the letter announcing the availability of an appointment for Lung had come only the day before, after a long wait, and it was too late for the Thursday convoy. We were too anxious to wait another week. We had learned to do things spontaneously in Vietnam, since there was no guaranteed tomorrow.

Lung and I waited by the main entrance to the Victory Hotel compound while Roderick and Sergeant Dinh went for the jeep. A large weeping willow tree shaded us from the bright sun. Lung looked up at the tree. "Trung Shi Davis says this is weeping tree. You have the same in America?"

"Yes we do," I said. "It's a graceful tree which grows very quickly. We call it a willow, weeping willow because its leaves appear sometimes to be drops of water, like tears." Lung looked at the large tree in silence.

To avoid being ordered directly not to go, we took the jeep without asking. Roderick Davis was armed with an M-16, Dinh with an M-79 grenade launcher. Each had a bandoleer of ammunition. I wore a Colt .45 automatic. With no helmets or flak vests, we packed Lung in the back seat and headed off in the direction of Saigon before anyone could say no. None of us was due to patrol on the river until the following Monday, and Lowell Webb, the section commander, had agreed to do my pre-patrol morning briefs while we were absent. "Just don't tell me where you're going," the lieutenant had said the night before we left. The risk was small, especially if we drove quickly, as there was no advance planning or coordination. The scheduled weekly convoys were periodically ambushed anyway. Lung was terrified as we drove out of My Tho in the jeep, with Sergeant Dinh riding shotgun.

We left for Saigon at first light and were more than halfway there before we were forced to slow down. "We've made good time so far, Sir," Roderick said, looking at his watch. "We've averaged forty miles an hour, a record on Highway 4."

The dusty green jeep, with canvas canopy down and windshield up, slowed for the crowded buses and three-wheeled cyclos clogging the road. Near the fifty-kilometer marker, Sergeant Dinh began to get nervous. He was an experienced fighter, born in the northern provinces of Vietnam, who had fought the French as a Vietminh. After the battle of Dien Bien Phu and the Geneva Accords, Dinh had taken his family south, where he fought in the South Vietnamese rangers until badly wounded in the hip. After rehabilitation, he ended up with the river police in My Tho, where he lived with his wife and two teen-aged children. Dinh was one of the older river police who rode the American boats. He was reliable, but nervous under fire.

Dinh's champion was the thirteenth century Vietnamese general and father of guerrilla tactics, Tran Hung Dao, who had led an army of 200,000 against the Kublai Kahn's invading force of more than 500,000 Mongols. Outnumbered and initially defeated, General Tran Hung Dao resisted his emperor's order to surrender, saying, "If your majesty wishes to surrender, please first cut off my head." Thus, with restored confidence, the emperor ordered continued resistance. The general rekindled the flagging spirit of the Vietnamese and had the words "Kill Mongols" tattooed on his soldier's arms. He then led his army of Vietnamese to victory as the leader of one of very few peoples to defeat the Mongols tactically. Sergeant Dinh, like many soldiers fighting the Vietcong, had the words, "Sat Cong"—"kill communists"—tattooed on his upper arm in memory of General Tran Hung Dao.

The traffic had slowed to nearly a crawl and Dinh jumped out of the jeep. "Dai Ui, I have look-see what problem." He disappeared for about five minutes and suddenly emerged from a gaggle of Vietnamese laborers hunkered down by the side of the road, smoking and chewing betel nut. Dinh, even more nervous, jumped back in the jeep. "Dai Ui, beaucoup VC," he said and pointed ahead. "Roadblock, many traffic. Must go back."

Roderick and I were taking turns driving and I was at the wheel. Roderick sat in the shotgun seat with the M-79, Dinh in the back seat with Lung, cradling his M-16. "Let's have a look." I swung the jeep onto the dirt shoulder and increased speed up the left side of the highway, dodging stalled vehicles, until we came to a large bus sitting in the center of the road, about one hundred meters ahead. Vietnamese were scurrying off the bus and heading into the bush on both sides of the road. There were at least fifty meters of clearing on either side of the highway before the treeline started. The cleared strip provided decent visibility on both flanks. It was not the most dangerous stretch of the road. We had already passed the segment called "ambush alley" more than fifteen kilometers earlier, where the treeline reached the edge of the road. But the Vietnamese had an uncanny ability to foresee danger, and when they began to disappear from the scene it usually meant something serious was about to happen.

I decided it was foolish at this point to turn back through ambush alley. The best tactic would be to charge ahead, making as difficult a target as possible. With the heavy traffic ahead on the road, it was unlikely there would be mines.

"Hold on," I shouted, and stepped on the gas. The jeep shot out of the line and tore up the left lane, passing the stalled traffic. Suddenly, about thirty yards ahead, we saw a roadblock. Several trees lay across the road, and some brush was piled high in the middle. One small cyclo had gone into the ditch on the left, but there appeared to be enough room to pass. Hunkered down behind the wheel, I swerved to the left of the roadblock and sped ahead. For a fleeting moment, the rear end of the jeep began to slide off the road, skidding toward the ditch. As we drew abreast of the brush in the roadblock we saw it was not manned, but there could be Vietcong still in the adjacent area. It was not unusual for new roadblocks to appear at first light. It was the Vietcong's way of signalling to the local population that they still controlled the night.

With the jeep no more than twenty yards past the roadblock, three sharp cracks suddenly rang out in succession. The mirror on the driver's side of the jeep shattered, but the other rounds went astray. "Stay down," I shouted, and floored the accelerator. We started to skid and lost the left rear wheel into the ditch. With both rear wheels spinning, I tried to shift into four-wheel drive, but to my horror I stalled the engine. In the grim silence that followed an eternity seemed to go by. I leaned forward, pushed in the clutch, shifted into first, and turned the ignition switch so hard it snapped off in my hand. I quickly jerked the kay-bar knife from its holder between the front seats, and jammed its point into the small indentation left where the ignition had been.

Some early jeeps had ignition switches which did not require keys, for in a field situation the overriding requirement was reliability, not security. We worried less about having a jeep stolen than in having the ability to start it at any time without a key. Besides, there were other ways to lock a jeep. In My Tho, to prevent midnight requisitioners from making off with our jeeps, we would unscrew the single nut holding the steering wheel in place and carry the wheel with us. It was difficult to steer a jeep without a steering wheel unless one had a pipe wrench or strong teeth.

I took a deep breath and turned the knife. After what seemed like an endless pause, with every sound in the vicinity magnified, the engine roared to life. I eased out the clutch and the jeep lurched out of the ditch, into the center of the road, skidded sideways, broached nearly across the road, skidded straight, and screeched forward, leaving a cloud of dust and debris. A few more shots rang out, but no one saw where they hit. Slamming the gears out of four-wheel drive, we careened off another stalled and empty bus, leaving a dark green streak of jeep-paint before continuing down the road. We roared on for at least three kilometers before slowing to a safe speed.

"Everybody okay?" I looked around with a grin, but I was beginning to shake in delayed reaction.

"Okay here Boss," answered Davis, who had twisted around in his seat and was checking on Lung who was on the floor in the back underneath Sergeant Dinh, her crutches poking out at odd angles between the sergeant's legs. "Only casualty in the back seems to be Dinh's shorts," laughed Roderick. "He'll probably have to change 'em after that. Lung's okay." The mirror appeared to be the only loss, though we later discovered another bullet hole in the left front fender. The four of us, relieved to be alive, soared into Saigon, a city choking on its own traffic at the height of rush hour.

The roads were clogged with traffic: jeeps, old cars (many French, some American from the fifties, with wide fins and ridiculous looking chromed features), cyclos, motorscooters, and bicycles by the thousands. Women with au-dais flying rode the bicycles deftly, with the long trailing silk dress bottoms tucked neatly under their seats. I had been in Saigon only once before, upon my arrival four months earlier, and had to rely on Dinh's directions to find 70 Ba Huyen Than Quan, the World Rehabilitation Fund Center. We drove on, mixed in the stifling traffic like fish caught in a trap but forced to flow with the current.

We finally arrived, with our throats parched by the heat and exhaust fumes of the busy capital. Although it was frustrating to drive in Saigon, the city itself was alive with activity and filled with excitement. There was a breathless bustle in the city, as if it were finishing up a long run, and unable to quite catch its breath. Time seemed limited in Saigon, a city in constant panic, and no one was in charge of the chaos. Important looking American jeeps and staff cars sped around town, and Vietnamese generals in black sedans raced by with blinking lights and horns blaring. But no one escaped the snarled traffic which reduced everything to the lowest common denominator—getting to a destination.

We climbed out of the jeep, stretched, and brushed off our clothes. Sergeant Dinh straightened Lung's au-dai, bought especially for the occasion, and untangled her crutches from the back seat. Dinh remained behind with the weapons and jeep, as the rest of us walked into the large building, which resembled a villa in the very smart, up-market neighborhood. Inside, a Vietnamese receptionist greeted us cordially and ushered us in. We were a strange looking party, two fatigue-clad men in black berets and a young

Vietnamese child in a light blue au-dai with white trousers beneath. The long trousers hid the fact that young Lung had only one foot; she was becoming remarkably agile on the crutches.

"We'll bring you something to drink. There are toilets across the hall." The receptionist smiled politely, but stared at Lung. Vietnamese children, especially urchins from the rice paddies, seldom received such attention.

A tall, slender Vietnamese woman entered from a side entrance to the terrace.

"You may call me Yen. I am chief administrator for the section dealing with artificial limbs for young people." She spoke impeccable English, and ushered us up a flight of stairs onto a large terrace filled with potted palms, vases, and elegant polished chairs, each next to a porcelain elephant. A young Vietnamese boy appeared carrying glasses of cool lemonade. Yen spoke in a soft voice, explaining, "I learned English in California."

She outlined the procedure. Lung would have to remain at the center for several days for fitting. Lung's countenance fell when Yen told her that her bed was in a room on another floor and that she would make sure Lung was returned safely to My Tho after the procedure. Lung was unhappy at the prospect of staying alone in Saigon and stared at the floor as Roderick and I said good-bye. "Don't worry, she will be fine here. I can send word to you in My Tho when she is ready to come back. We will ensure she gets some therapy and training on the new limb." Yen escorted us downstairs and again told us not to worry. "French doctor Henri Pelosof is aware of the case and will give it his full attention," Yen assured us.

After leaving the Rehabilitation Center, I had Dinh direct us to the navy river squadron office in U.S. naval headquarters. I had unfinished business with the administrative commander of the river patrol force, Commander Kane. Four months before, when reporting into the same headquarters, I had been promised command of my own river section, and had subsequently been assigned to the

My Tho section of 532. I would take advantage of this rare opportunity to be in Saigon to stump for my own command. I met the commander, who appeared not only to have forgotten his words of four months ago, but even who I was and where I was stationed. After some embarrassed shuffling, the kindly, but stuffy old commander made some notes and excused himself to go to the morning briefing for Rear Admiral Veth, then Chief NAVFORV.

The navy never changed, I thought as Petty Officer Davis and I wandered together through the corridors of headquarters, enjoying the cool air generated by the fans rotating in the heat. Young officers in starched combat greens raced with pointers and briefing slides from their air conditioned offices to the briefing room. There were maps everywhere and the standard U.S. navy prints of past wars hung in dusty frames on the walls. The appearance of two sailors from an operational river section seemed an embarrassment to the NAVFORV staff and as we tried to make conversation, most of the headquarters people ducked away, ashamed of their creature comforts of air conditioning, steaming hot navy coffee, long lunches, and evening happy hours spent in the clubs scattered around Saigon.

At headquarters it almost seemed that there was no war. Saigon offices closed for the weekend every Friday at five o'clock, and the Saigon warriors went on about their lives as if serving in the Pentagon; only the dress was different. It was easy for us to be cocky when in town from the operational units, and we could not help but marvel at the differences in duty. In My Tho and on the river there was the constant reality of combat. In Saigon it seemed that the war would go away whenever a senior officer gave the order.

We returned to the jeep to find Sergeant Dinh somehow sleeping on top of the weapons. We had all been on the river the entire night before leaving My Tho, and though exhausted, we took the jeep for a run around Saigon just to see the action. We drove down Tu Do Street, the main thoroughfare, and saw Americans everywhere, in

tropical shirts and slacks, Vietnamese girls in tow. Uniforms domi-
nated, and there were gaily lit bars every few feet. We saw a Holly-
wood Bar, a New York Bar, and every imaginable lure of night life.
Dinh disapproved of the scene and looked sullen the entire time.

The beautiful Co Yen from the Rehabilitation Center had given
us the name of a restaurant that was a favorite of the Rehabilitation Center staff. We found the address, hid the jeep on a side
street, and entered a brightly lit, well-appointed restaurant, with
waiters in white jackets and wicker tables with candles. It was
about nine o'clock when we arrived, and feeling a little self-con-
scious in our uniforms, we sat in a corner at a small table. The
waiter brought wine and beer and a small plate of Vietnamese egg
rolls with a saucer of nuc mam. As we sat enjoying the cool breeze
blowing through the open terrace, we could see a separate room
with a large round table crowded with foreigners. As we drank the
French red wine in silence, I noticed some guests at the other table
were speaking German, others English, and some French. There
were also several Vietnamese men and women. The conversation
in the adjoining room grew louder as the evening passed. There
were few others in the restaurant except for the crowd at the
round table and the three of us from My Tho.

Suddenly a figure appeared at the step leading into the larger
room. A middle-aged man in a tropical white suit looked over at us
and asked in an unmistakable New England accent, "Is one of you
Lieutenant Huchthausen by any chance?"

Amazed to hear my name in English, I rose and greeted the gen-
tleman. "I heard about your case from the Rehabilitation Center's
Dr. Pelosof and Co Yen who are here in the next room. I'm with the
agriculture section of AID at the American Embassy. Please join us.
We have a reporter from United Press International (UPI) who's in-
terested in your story and would like to meet you." The man in
white introduced himself and his wife as Mr. and Mrs. Joe Hamilton. They knew the others from the Rehabilitation Center and

brought us into the side room. "These are the two gentlemen who brought in the little girl from My Tho today."

The others at the table listened in silence as Joe Hamilton described in detail the events surrounding our presence. After telling the story and receiving nods and murmurs of approval, the conversation again broke up into fragmented groups. I noticed Co Yen sitting at the other end of the table and I rose to greet her. She, in turn, introduced me to a reporter from UPI, and another young reporter from New York who expressed an interest in the story of Lung, and pressed for more details. "Where's your unit stationed, Lieutenant?"

"South of here in Dinh Thuong Province. Takes about four hours by road if you're not delayed by traffic."

"We'd like to come down and do a story on the girl, if you don't mind."

"Sure, we'll be back there tomorrow. Come on down. You can ask for me or Lieutenant Webb, the section commander. Here, I'll show you how to find us in My Tho." I explained how to get to the Victory Hotel and the PBR base. Joe Hamilton invited us to join them, but I declined, mentioning our plans for an early departure for My Tho the next day. The Hamiltons, apparently moved by the story, were eager to help Lung.

"If you need a place for her, she can stay with us. We live very close to the Rehabilitation Center. We have two young daughters, and Lung may feel more comfortable with a family than in a hospital."

"That's very kind, Mr. Hamilton."

"Leave the details to us. Miss Yen can see to it that Lung is brought to us after her therapy and fitting. We'll make sure she returns to my My Tho."

I looked at Yen before leaving. She returned my glance, then lowered her eyes—a sign of fine manners and traditional Vietnamese modesty. "I can't thank you enough for your help."

"You're quite welcome, Lieutenant. We don't often get officers from the field here on cases with children. You see, in Vietnam, only a man's own children are important to him. Children in the countryside are becoming independent because the war has taken away their normal safety net, as you call it in the states. These children someday will show the results. I just hope they stand up well."

"I guess it just hurts us to see all this going on, and to see the kids suffer so much. No one's ever there to hold their hands."

"Our children are strong, but only the future will tell if they are strong enough."

I was moved by this young woman, who although in her midtwenties, looked like a teenager. She had grace and charm of a sophisticated woman, and the fresh face of a young farm girl. "Lung's become important to our men down there in the delta. She's grown into a kind of mascot, a tangible result of our time here. I'd appreciate it if you'd look after her."

"I will. I promise." Yen said as she lowered her eyes. We said good-bye to the group, and the reporter followed me to the door. He agreed to travel to My Tho to cover Lung's story and the U.S. Navy's role in her rescue. Yen came to the door, and as we parted, I took her hand. "Thanks again for your help." While looking at her, I sensed that Yen's involvement in Lung's life might be more important than we knew at the time.

Lung's strong will was shown later after Roderick, Dinh, and I left her in the teeming capital. After her meeting with the doctor, and terrified of spending the first night in the city, she fled the center and made her way back to My Tho alone on a crowded bus. After arriving in My Tho, Lung showed up at the navy compound, determined not to return to Saigon. Co Thuong took her back to Saigon the next day in an army shuttle helicopter. This time she stayed, completed the therapy while staying with the Hamiltons, and with her new leg, returned to her studies at the Catholic school. The UPI reporter turned up in My Tho several days after our return and took a series of photos, which appeared in my hometown newspaper in upstate New York and in the center spread of the New York Daily News. We had no idea how the action of the reporter would affect Lung's future.

*   *   *

Someone who played a major part in the life of Lung from the day she was brought to the hospital, was the "Dragon Lady," twenty-eight-year-old Thieu Bich Thuong. The daughter of a wealthy family in Ben Tre, Co Thuong had been educated in France and spoke fluent English, French, and German. She had worked initially for the province headquarter's American advisory office, and then for the U.S. Naval Intelligence liaison officer in the tri-province areas of Dinh Toung, Go Cong, and Ben Tre. A strong-willed lady, Co Thuong soon elevated herself from the official position of interpreter/translator, to deputy to the reluctant liaison officer, who could not cope with Thuong's aggressive behavior. She was a tough Vietnamese woman who knew how to take advantage of the American male's propensity to give ground when confronted by a strong oriental female, especially when weak in the language skills. The American navy liaison officer depended on her during dealings with entrenched Vietnamese bureaucrats. Co Thuong became a symbol of the mystique in which Americans held Vietnamese who were in positions of authority.

Thuong was supportive of Lung, assisted the sailors in equipping her with a modest wardrobe, helped her to enroll in the Catholic school, and generally did things the awkward, but well-meaning Americans could not do. Thuong became a fixture in the navy Victory Hotel compound and was present at most planning operations, ostensibly to assist in coordinating with local Vietnamese forces. Co Thuong appeared to be helpful in every way, almost too helpful, until the Tet Offensive. She then mysteriously disappeared.

Another colorful My Tho character who played a regular part in Lung's life was the elderly Phan Van Phu, the barber, bartender, and odd-jobs man at the U.S. Army advisory compound. It was Phu who had assisted Roderick Davis in constructing the first set of crude wooden crutches for Lung when she first left the My Tho hospital. Old Mr. Phu told stories about the days of the French, the Japanese, and again the French after their return in 1945. A devout Buddhist who had spent time in jail during both the French and Japanese occupations, Mr. Phu knew all the senior Americans in town. He cut their hair, fixed them drinks at cocktail time, coordinated their laundry and the cleaning of their barracks, and generally helped out around the compound. Jokes about his loyalty never seriously brought his character into doubt.

*   *   *

The visit in Saigon with the River Squadron Headquarters paid off. I received a call two months later directing that I detach from the My Tho section and report to Sa Dec on 1 October to relieve Lieutenant Joe Martin of duties as commander of River Section 513, the sole PBR unit on the Cu Long, upper Mekong, responsible for the river from Sa Dec, seventy miles north, and west to the Cambodian border. The entire face of my Vietnam experience changed dramatically with this transfer.

Lung, now moving nimbly on her new leg, continued on in the Catholic school. I said good-bye to her and Roderick, who remained with the My Tho river unit, and made my way northwest to Sa Dec. During the three months preceding Tet, I visited Lung several times.

Once in January, still before Tet, Lung hitched a ride on one of our patrol boats returning to Sa Dec from maintenance work in My Tho. She stayed for several days and while in Sa Dec, traveled with our boats to some of the outlying villages where the work of liaison and protective coordination continued with the local, regional and popular forces. Once she accompanied us on a patrol to Kien Van District to visit with Dai Ui Chuk, and the American advisor, Major Don Marnon.

Nguyen Van Chuk was one of the fiercest fighters in the South Vietnamese Army and district chief of Kien Van. Born in North Vietnam, he fought as a young man with the Vietminh against the French. A devout Catholic, he left the north during Operation "Passage to Freedom" aboard the USS *Montrose*, part of U.S. Navy Task Force 90, the American effort to assist the evacuation of Vietnamese civilians and military personnel from North Vietnam following the French defeat at Dien Bien Phu and the Geneva Accords of July, 1954.

Chuk made the trip wounded and alone only to begin his new life in another war. A wiry and fearless combatant, he became district chief in the delta town of Kien Van, following years of combat against the Vietcong. His wife was a delta woman from My Tho, who had been educated in Catholic schools and spoke French and English. They had two beautiful daughters. Chuk was an aggressive leader who believed in the principles of democracy and independence. His motivations were curious. A strong Christian, he was opposed in principle to Communism, yet dreamed of a united Vietnam, free from foreign domination with a market economy open to foreign investors. Chuk was close to his American advisors, and spent many long hours debating the blessings of a democratic society which would possess the traditions of strict Chinese culture and ancient Annamite discipline.

While most American advisors had to coax and encourage their Vietnamese counterparts into more aggressive action in the field, Chuk was constantly leading the Americans on night ambush patrols and operations he devised to force contact with the local Vietcong. Well known for his spirited and aggressive leadership, the Vietcong targeted Chuk for elimination, but failed to either kill him or to permanently overrun his district headquarters.

The navy river patrol force spent much time and effort defending Chuk's district seat located just three kilometers north of the Cua Tieu main channel of the Mekong. His ideals were firmly based on the traditions of Vietnamese resistance, first against the Chinese, then against the French and the Japanese. He viewed the American presence as one of temporary necessity. He had despised the weak leadership of South Vietnam ever since the seduction of Bao Dai by the French in the post-World War II years. He abhorred the exploitation of the Vietnamese during the French colonial period by other wealthy Vietnamese. They were the worst parasites, operating against the ideals of freedom and private enterprise. Chuk was of Chinese origin, although a true Vietnamese patriot. The tragedy of his life was that he was caught up in the process of uniting Vietnam, a cause which he supported but ended up fighting against, because of the means that were adopted to achieve the end. In the end, Chuk was unable to support his own goals because they were the same ones espoused by the communists, whom he opposed and despised.

During the months preceding Tet, Chuk had a sense that the worst lay ahead. With his American Army counterpart, Major Don Marnon, he had devised a support plan with the navy river section in Sa Dec, located a short twenty-minute run across the river, for an automatic defense if attacked by the Vietcong. His district headquarters was located approximately one kilometer off the main river at the junction of two canals, which met and flowed directly to the main river where it formed a perfect Y. The 1,000-meter flow to the main river cut through a field of flat land which was kept shorn of its normal high grass covering. This afforded the PBRs an unobstructed view from the water. They could dash in off the main river, take up supporting positions in the two branches of the Y, and provide a curtain of deadly covering heavy machine gun fire around the main outpost of sector headquarters. Thus, if attacked, the river boats could enter the main canal in relative safety due to the lack of cover for VC forces seeking to ambush and cut them off. The boats could sit in the Y and protect the outpost until air or artillery cover relieved them. Chuk and Don Marnon had built a high watchtower over the compound and installed a heavy machine gun, loaned by the river navy, to give added protection and early warning to the outpost.

During the January visit, Dai Ui Chuk took us to his home in the village, which was located along the main canal leading to the river. His wife laid out a rich spread of Vietnamese food in honor of our visit with Lung. Their two daughters, ages six and eight, were delighted with Lung's presence. The atmosphere was family-like as the American advisors, Don Marnon, his lieutenant and two sergeants, the river sailors with Chuk, and his district staff of Vietnamese officers, joined in a lunch of river crab and large tom xu, the renowned delta shrimp which grew up to three inches long and were delicious, especially when dipped into a sauce of nuc mam, garlic, and hot peppers. There was chicken, pork, greens of every description, and large bowls of rice, plump and sticky. Bottles of Ba Mui Ba (33) beer stood on the table, still flecked with rice husks from the ice house nearby, where chunks of ice were kept in deep holes lined with rice husks for insulation. There were bottles of homemade sweet rice wine and the stronger bassi-de, a clear, distilled rice liquor, which smelled like gasoline, tasted like grass, and had the kick not unlike vodka. The PBR sailors provided C-ration cookies and jams for dessert. There was fruit of every description: mango, papaya, breadfruit, banana, pineapple, and star fruit. The Vietnamese were able, with their extraordinary warmth and congeniality, to provide a rich banquet to their American friends with foods which came from no further away than the local market and river. The young Chuk daughters sang the local songs, and Lung recited the traditional Vietnamese poem of the rice cycle, popular with all the delta children:

> The twelfth moon for potato growing,
> the first for beans, the second for eggplant.
> In the third, we break the land

to plant rice in the fourth while rains are strong.
The man plows, the woman plants,
and in the fifth: the harvest, and the gods are good
—From *A Farmer's Calendar*

Lung stayed in Sa Dec for several days and, as suddenly as she had appeared, packed her string bag and announced her intended return to My Tho and school. I took her to the river and put her on a water taxi heading southeast to Vinh Long and My Tho. As we said good-bye, Lung looked up and smiled.

"Good-bye, Dai Ui." She said as she disappeared onto the crowded wooden boat. It was January, 1968, the last time I saw Lung in Vietnam.

Tet is the most important of Vietnam's ancient holidays and marks the lunar New Year. It is a time to return to the home village, to visit the tombs of relatives and temples with humility and thankfulness. Debts are to be paid and errors of life corrected. Prayers are traditionally offered for the good health and success of loved ones in the new year.

—*Vietnamese Folklore Calendar*

Peter

Some historians consider the Tet Offensive a great victory, others call it a resounding defeat for the Vietcong and North Vietnamese. Still others claim it was a thorough triumph for U.S. troops, yet a humiliating setback for America. For the American navy's river patrol force in the delta in 1968, the Tet Offensive marked the end of the long period when we operated on the rivers and canals of the upper Mekong with only sporadic contact with the enemy. After the start of the long offensive, we experienced much more frequent contact with the Vietcong and the inherent bloodshed and loss of life that already characterized the war farther north. After Tet the situation changed to a three-month period of protracted fighting on the rivers. It was then I learned that physical fear does not compare with the dread a commander feels when he considers the unthinkable: failing the men with whose confidence he is entrusted.

Lung

The Catholic boarding school on Hien Vuong Street had become a real home for me. I felt more welcome there than at my cousin's home near the My Tho market where I had first tried to work fol-

73

lowing release from the hospital. I could not keep up with the other fruit sellers at the market, and I could not move fast enough to keep out of the way of the young boys who sometimes stole my fruit and ran away, or tripped me when I walked carrying the large cans of cooking oil from the boat landing to the market.

At the school, I was accepted by the other students despite my leg. I liked the quiet of morning worship in the big church. The sisters were friendly and helpful. The food was good and plentiful, and I began to read and write, and to study English and French. Phuong, the kind Catholic sister, was my best friend. She helped me a great deal, and found two roommates for me who also became my friends.

On weekends, I went to the American Victory Hotel to visit Trung Shi Davis and Dai Ui Peter if they were there. The sailors were nice to me, practiced their Vietnamese language with me, laughed, and sometimes acted silly. Co Thuong, the interpreter, was also helpful. She taught me how to act and when to leave the compound and return to school so I was not a nuisance. The sailors were often too busy to relax and sometimes returned from the river in dark moods. I sat for hours just to listen to the Americans talk. Sometimes they were very friendly and other times, in their dark moods, they were cold and mean. I figured it was the war and the fighting that made them that way. Co Thuong told me to disappear when they acted sad.

In October, Dai Ui Peter moved to Sa Dec. After he left, I visited the Victory less. Sometimes Trung Shi Davis came to see me at the school and brought me gifts. My Tho was then mostly quiet and peaceful. Sometimes at night we heard shooting near town, but it did not reach our school which was set back behind the pretty palm trees and away from the busy road. Those were happy times. One night, following our celebration of the Lunar New Year, everything changed.

On the night of Tet, after the evening meal, we went to prayer and then to bed. I remember it was noisy outside and there were fireworks everywhere in My Tho. The exploding fireworks frightened me because they were just like the sounds in my village of Phu Duc when the foot-soldiers came. It was too noisy to sleep, so I thought of the river and trees near Phu Duc, my brothers, and my mother. I hoped they were not scared and that everything would be all right.

I must have gone to sleep, for the next thing I knew the whole earth was shaking. There were loud explosions everywhere. My roommates were sitting up and looking scared. There was another loud crack, a blinding light, and the sound of many insects flying in our room. A choking smoke engulfed us. We heard Phuong's voice shouting for us to get up and go downstairs. I tried to find my plastic leg. I always put it on the floor by the bed at night so I would not lose it, but because of the smoke I could not find it. I crawled around feeling beside and under the bed, but the smoke was too thick to see. My eyes burned. I crawled toward the corner where my old crutches were kept, but I could not find them either. The smell from the smoke was terrible and burned my throat.

One of my roommates, Dang, helped me to the doorway just as Phuong ran by again shouting for us to move quickly. She took me by the arm and led me to the stairway. There was another blinding flash and a noise so loud it tore at my ears. Phuong fell down, but got up quickly, picked me up in her arms, and stumbled for the stairway. Together we half walked and half fell down the stairs. At the bottom, Phuong fell again, and then pushed me under the staircase, and told me to stay there and pray. Then she disappeared. I crouched under the stairs for a long time. I was so frightened I shook like a tree in a storm.

Time stood still as I waited. I could see dark figures running past the open gates when I put my head down near the floor. Two forms slipped inside the gate and ran silently, close to the wall by the courtyard. They had slim bodies, carried long weapons, and did not wear uniforms. I knew by their silence that they were Vietcong. I froze, barely able to breathe. I then heard a popping noise, the same as we heard the day I was hit on the river. One dark figure put a long thin weapon to his shoulder and fired something out into the street. Then he slipped behind a pillar on the terrace where I could hear his breath coming in short, sharp gasps. There was a loud thud from the street and a flash illuminated the whole school.

I curled up more tightly, trying not to be seen. The shooting continued as several Vietcong soldiers scampered through the gates and hid in the schoolyard. One came within a few meters of my staircase and knelt down, breathing very heavily. Luckily, he could not fit under the stairs where I was—the space was too small. He rested awhile, and seemed paralyzed. How long he was there I could not say. It may have been an hour. Eventually he rolled over and relieved himself on the staircase. I wanted to move away but I dared not. I hardly breathed at all. I thought of anything pleasant, like the small birds in Phu Duc and the wide river which always made me feel calm. The man, now no more than a few centimeters away, was as still, as if asleep. The two of us sat in the quiet for what seemed like hours. I thought of distant beautiful things, as Mother had taught me, to calm myself and to remove my mind from the present dangers surrounding me. My thoughts returned to the American sailors, how kind and gentle they were in their coarse way, how they always seemed to notice me when no one else did, and how they made me feel important without being condescending. Davis and Dai Ui Peter talked to me in the same tone and inflection they used when speaking to other sailors, and that puzzled me. How strange the Americans were!

Suddenly, I began to panic. What if this Vietcong soldier, not an arm's reach away, could see or read my thoughts? Could he tell I was thinking of the Americans? Surely he would notice and kill me. I shivered and tried to concentrate on the thought of the fish stakes in the canal near our village. I was afraid to think of anything else. The picture of the fish stakes made me feel at home. I knew them well, had seen them nearly every day of my earlier life, and played amidst them with my brothers and cousin Din. We used to catch the fish already trapped in the nets beneath the water and sneak them home to our mother, pretending to have caught them in our own nets on the ends of our long fishing poles.

The dark figures in the courtyard stiffened and flattened themselves against the ground. There was a rattle and the sound of a motor clanking down the main street. A burst of shooting erupted and the dark figures began to roll in unison toward the edge of the courtyard. The soldier crouching close to me let out a groan and rolled toward the low wall surrounding the terrace, where two porcelain pots stood holding plants. There was a deafening roar as the courtyard erupted in white light. I saw two of the black figures fly through the air, their arms outstretched, and land like rag dolls on the ground. The heat and the shock of the blast took my breath away. I curled up tightly, closed my eyes, and prayed.

When I opened my eyes, I could see the courtyard again bathed in a bright light coming from an object swinging in the air. I glanced cautiously at the soldier still lying close to me, and saw he was a young man, no older than my oldest brother. He looked frightened and was poised to run somewhere. But he did not move. He looked directly at me. I was sure he could see me in the dazzling light. I saw he was looking through me, as if in deep thought. He looked dazed as he raised his weapon and ran out into the street. A large metal object roared into life like a moving fortress. The machine started shooting and cut the young Vietcong in half as he ran. I shuddered and closed my eyes again, imagining that he was my brother. I made myself as small as I could and waited. Nothing helped me stop shaking, until the clamor faded. Day came, and I stayed where I was.

The sound of the explosions shifted across the street to the Thien Mau Home for orphans and the retired. I stayed under the stairs and waited for Phuong to come back, but she never did. I stayed there until it got dark. I had nothing to eat or drink all day.

Still I waited. Finally some other students came by and said we had to leave the school and go home. But I did not want to move until I heard from Phuong that it was all right. I asked one girl from my French language class if she knew where Phuong was. She looked at me and began to cry. She said Phuong was lying hurt in the courtyard. The girl then ran away.

It was still dark when I got up and hopped to the courtyard. As I approached I saw a group of students and several sisters standing around Phuong. The priest was sitting on the ground holding her up by the shoulders. My roommate, Dang, was by me then. We looked in horror at Phuong and the priest. Phuong's face was an unrecognizable mass of blood. Father told us all to run home while it was still dark, and to avoid the main street. He looked at me and sighed.

"Lung, go to the river. If you can get to the river you'll be safe. Go now, my child. God be with you."

Dang whispered to me to stay where I was, and she disappeared. I was wondering what to do as I watched the others vanish into the darkness. Father told me to hurry up and start running. I told him I could not run because my leg was missing. He shouted at several other students who were too scared to run away. I waited, not wanting to leave, and yet wishing to do what the priest asked. I began to make my way toward the gate when Dang returned. She had found my plastic leg and helped me strap it on.

Together we ran through the courtyard, out the front gates, and down the side of the main street. A fire glowed from across the street at the orphanage. Smoke was everywhere. Dang shouted to hurry up, but I turned to look back at the school. It was burning. The roof over our rooms had collapsed. The church, too, had lost most of its roof and was still smoking. I wanted to cry, but was unable. My stomach hurt, and my eyes stung. I sat on the ground by a tree and waited to catch my breath. As I tried to run, I began falling over things lying in the way. I crawled behind a high concrete wall to rest.

I must have fallen asleep, because when I opened my eyes, it was starting to get light. Everything looked grey, and I was cold. My white cotton trousers were wet, and my white blouse was hardly white anymore. I waited until it was a little lighter, then began to walk slowly down the side of Hien Vuong Street. Suddenly, I fell over something lying in the road. I felt to see what it was. It was a dead man, horribly disfigured. Only his face was free of blood. I looked and saw his eyes open as if staring at the trees above. I quickly got up and ran towards the side street. I saw more people running now, two women and some more young people. I tried my best to keep steady, but I fell often.

There were more bodies lying on the ground. There was blood everywhere, and the air smelled sweet, like incense and smoke. I kept going, weaving down the side streets toward the park at the foot of the boulevard. Loud popping started back near the school as I worked my way down to the park. I saw the daylight reflected in the river. It was like a warm embrace, and seemed like the only part of the world not transformed into ugly chaos. I somehow knew that if I reached the riverbank I would survive.

I kept going, soon reaching the landing where the water taxis loaded and unloaded. There were more and more people arriving. I was jostled and pushed in the crowd, but kept in the middle of the group as it moved toward a line of boats bobbing at the embankment. I pushed and shoved until I reached the nearest boat. I tried to step over the side but could not quite get my leg over the edge. I fell into the water.

Suddenly, I was yanked into mid-air. A strong arm lowered me into the boat. When I recovered my footing, I looked up and saw the face of a Vietnamese soldier above me. He pushed me further into the boat, and onto a seat on the far side nearest the water. He then shouted for the boat to push off since there were already too many people in the boat. Several people and packages fell into the river, but the boat succeeded in pulling free of the crowd and into the main channel. The soldier stood behind me. I noticed he was bleeding from a wound in his side. He sat down next to me and went to sleep.

The boat kept going across the river, where most people got off. I stayed on because the soldier was leaning on me so hard I could not get up. I did not want to wake him, since he had saved me from being pushed in the water. After several more stops, I recognized the island near Phu Duc my home village. I was still unable to move from my seat. The boatman reached forward, pulled the soldier off of me, and I stood to climb out of the boat. I stepped onto the mud bank and managed to crawl up the landing to the cool earth on top. I looked back at the water taxi and saw that the soldier had slumped to the bottom of the boat, his eyes were staring up into the sky.

I turned and began to walk back to my village. It was quiet again, and I was warm for the first time. I wondered how my brothers would look since I had not seen them in a long time. How would I explain why I was so dirty?

Peter

To River Patrol Section 513 on the upper reaches of the Mekong, operating out of Sa Dec, Tet was an intensification of the war but not completely without its advantages. For once, the enemy was out in force, and we were able to engage him on our terms. As I saw it, the whole Offensive, which for us lasted three months, was neither a victory nor a defeat for either side. The enemy just did things he had not done before, and we adapted readily to the new situation. We never speculated on the future or tried to interpret the greater meaning of the campaign. We lived from day to day: re-acted to calls for support for outposts under attack, conducted forced reconnaissance inside canals around Sa Dec, and helped the Ninth ARVN Division regain control of areas lost during the Vietcong attacks. We spent night and day on the river. We ate and slept in the boats returning only to fuel and replenish ammunition.

When the Tet Offensive began the morning of January 30, 1968, five of my Sa Dec unit's ten boats were operating on the Cambodian border with the executive officer, New Englander Lieutenant Bob Donovan and Master Chief Petty Officer Hoffman in charge. We occasionally staged operations from Sa Dec to the border at the request of the U.S. Army Special Forces commanders in Tan Chau and Chau Doc. Our PBRs provided the Special Forces the much-needed extra dimension of heavier, mobile fire power from the main river and canals. Our success rate in supporting the Special Forces camps was high. We helped them clear out strongholds from which the VC staged attacks on their camps and surrounding outposts.

To conduct operations in the border area (Red Dog Ops), we simply loaded the LCM-8 landing craft, called a "mike" boat, with a large rubber fuel bladder, spare ammunition, water and rations, and sailed north up the wide Mekong accompanied by five PBRs manned with volunteers. We took the standard C-rations—not to eat but to trade with the Vietnamese—for crab, fish, and rice. The PBR sailors subsisted primarily on the plentiful local food during the forays to the border areas. In return, the Vietnamese received the well loved American C-ration jam, cookies, canned scrambled eggs, beenie-weenies, and most of all, cigarettes.

By chance, we had a Red Dog Op already underway and anchored in mid-river off Tan Chau when the Offensive began. Bob Donovan's transit north was completed in time to assist the American and local forces in defending the town from fierce assault. Donovan's group of five Sa Dec PBRs later joined forces with a task force of SEALs and PBRs from the Bassac River, which were coincidentally conducting an interdiction operation called "Bold Dragon I" near Chau Doc, a major town and province capital on the Cambodian border, twenty miles to the southwest of Tan Chau.

After joining forces with the Bassac PBRs, Donovan and Chief Hoffman's segment of River Section 513 provided some welcomed mobile heavy fire support from the river as the Special Forces and Navy Seals fought a rear guard action to cover the evacuation of non-combatant Americans from Chau Doc. Bob Donovan later told of the unique experience of pouring 50-caliber fire into portions of the Chau Doc already overrun by the North Vietnamese and Vietcong forces. Donovan engaged from the main river at the request of beleaguered Americans still fighting in the town. He had formed the five PBRs into a line ahead, and raked the occupied areas with fire to enable the Americans to withdraw. As with most of the initial Vietcong and NVN successes during the Offensive, the territory won was held only temporarily, and later retaken by South Vietnamese and U.S. forces.

The Tet action at the home base of Sa Dec began early on the morning of the 30th when the Vietcong attacked the Ninth ARVN Division Headquarters, the American Army advisors' compound, and our PBR pier area with mortar and recoilless rifle fire. After the initial shellings, I scrambled my PBRs out to mid-river and nested them alongside the anchored mike boat, a far less vulnerable position than in the center of Sa Dec.

While Bob Donovan's half of the section of five boats was busy up north in support of the Army Special Forces at Tan Chau and Chau Doc, the second half of our section spent the weeks helping the Ninth ARVN Division re-establish its hold on the surrounding provinces. At the same time, unknown to me, Lung was in the midst of her ordeal in My Tho, where heavy fighting had erupted near her boarding school. We did not learn of the seriousness of the situation in My Tho until after the first month of the Offensive. There was action everywhere in the delta, and the PBR sailors were in the thick of it.

*   *   *

On the first night of the Offensive, our small operations center received the codeword call that Kien Van sector headquarters was under attack. I ordered the night patrol already on the river to execute our joint pre-planned relief operation in support of the Kien Van sector outpost and scrambled an additional boat so I could join the patrol on the river. We could now offer a three-boat defense of Dai Ui Chuk and his counterpart, American advisor Major Don Marnon. The outpost was under heavy ground attack.

The relief crew and I jumped into the jeep and headed toward the piers through the still sleeping town of Sa Dec. An uncanny tension filled the air as we threw our gear into the stand-by boat. The crew tore off the gun covers and charged the weapons while I made a fast radio check and vectored the patrol already out to a mid-river rendezvous. We cast off into the dark canal stream and headed toward the main river, not knowing what lay ahead.

When our single PBR joined the two-boat patrol already in mid-river, we made our way at top speed for the canal leading into the Kien Van headquarters. Nearing the canal, we could see flares hanging in the air and brilliant lines of red and gold tracer fire in the distance. As we approached the canal, we suddenly heard the sound of mortar rounds landing to the south of us in our own base town of Sa Dec. We heard them hit with their unmistakable *crump*, and hoped they had missed the town center at the pier area we had left behind. Turning up the volume of the radio, we listened in shocked disbelief as we strained to hear above the sound of the engine whine and pump scream. Sa Dec and several other district capitals were under simultaneous mortar attack. The predictions of a nationwide offensive, made by several Vietnamese river police and the naval intelligence summaries the week before, had been correct. A massive offensive was underway.

Our three-boat patrol, headed for the canal and not a half mile away, saw fires burning in the district town on the east side of the canal. There was no fire coming from the canal banks as we headed into the main canal toward the sub-sector headquarters compound. The three boats split on signal and took up station inside the Y. Now in radio contact with Don Marnon, we listened to his description of the situation on the ground. They were under sporadic mortar and B-40 rocket fire and had already repelled one sapper assault aimed at blowing a route through the thick barbed wire surrounding the outer rim of the compound. Don Marnon had stationed one American and a Vietnamese in the observation tower. The tower was coming under increasing sniper fire and unable to pinpoint any concentration of VC massing for another assault. Don asked us to hold fire until something developed.

Our boats were in the canals and in the Y where we had wide enough room to run in a racetrack pattern at good speed if careful not to run into the fish stakes or small piers. We cruised at a slow speed, completely darkened, ready to burst into full speed and fire at the first sign of shooting from the bank. The night was cool enough to make it necessary to wear foul weather gear under our flak jackets, and even then we were cold. Excitement was high, and the sound of gunfire and artillery coming from the direction of Sa Dec and south from the direction of Vinh Long gave the impression of a world plunging into a total war. The heavy darkness on the smooth river was the only comfort.

I listened to Don Marnon now whispering on the radio, indicating the vulnerability of his position inside the headquarters bunker. He had called for artillery, helo gunship, and "spooky" (C-47 gunship) support, but action elsewhere had all assets committed. There was no hope of assistance beyond the support of our three PBRs.

The *swoosh* of a rocket suddenly cut through the air followed by a flash, an explosion, and the sound of mortar rounds landing within the compound perimeter. Someone in the tower launched a flare as Don shouted over the radio, "Commence firing—they're in the wire!"

Both PBRs in the two branches of the Y opened fire and began to circle to create more difficult moving targets. They let out streams of waist-high 50-caliber fire around the compound, effectively seal-ing it off with a curtain of glowing tracers. My boat, which was in the middle, held fire and watched, ready to suppress any fire coming at the boats from the banks. For a brief moment there was quiet. An eerie feeling ran down my spine, as if I were staring directly into the face of an enemy at close range, one I could not see but only feel. I only hoped he could not see or smell me, as I remembered the Vietnamese claim that they could always smell Americans because of our diet. That night, in haste, I forgot to bring garlic cloves along to mask our odor. Then I worried that my dog tags might clatter together, although I had carefully taped them together. Then came the inevitable urge to relieve my bladder. All these worries built up as the silent moments ticked away.

Heavy fire burst simultaneously from both flanking boats; red tracers outlined the outpost perimeters precisely as planned. An abrupt flash followed by a roar came from one bank of the canal, preceding the yellow streak of a rocket fired at the northernmost boat. My third boat opened fire at the source. No other rounds followed.

The firing from the woods surrounding the outpost continued as the boats kept up a steady repetition of short bursts of machine gun fire. There was a momentary lull as Don Marnon shouted "cease fire" on the radio and conducted a quick recon to see what the situation was in the tower. He had lost contact with his two men and sent another two scrambling up the tower as the flare coverage ceased. There was a sudden burst of fire from the treeline, followed by several rocket firings. Another flare lit the sky. The tower received a direct hit and tilted at a crazy angle, as if ready to fall over. In the brief light one man could be seen clinging to the steep ladder rungs, another lay slumped on the rail at the top. Marnon quickly called for more fire.

"They're inside the perimeter—fire directly into the compound—we'll stay down." All three boats took the compound under direct fire and debris flew in all directions as the heavy 50-calibers decimated anything still moving in the compound. There was suddenly a huge explosion on the perimeter of the compound. Nothing came over the radio, and the three boats continued their fire, fearing the worst. After a pause of several minutes, a voice came over the radio, pleading with us to pour on the fire: "They're rushing the compound."

All three boats opened fire together. All nine 50-caliber machine guns sent a steady stream of uninterrupted fire into the compound. The 40-mm grenade launchers arched a stream of grenades into the outpost, now a cloud of dust and debris. Flares had ceased to come from the tower, so we fired hand flares from the center boat to illuminate the area. Eventually, the sounds of fire diminished as the first grey streaks of the morning sky spread over the compound. The three boats continued to circle as the sound of mortar fire decreased and came to an end. Don's voice came over the radio after an ominous pause.

"They're gone—withdrew. Cover us as soon as it's light enough. I'll go out to take a look." The minutes ticked by as the sky grew lighter. The acrid smell of smoke blew over the canals and the smell of the smoldering fires in the village hung in the air. The water lapped the sides of the boats, and the diesel engines purred in idle; a surreal quiet fell over the area.

A half-hour passed before Don signalled us to come ashore. I ordered the two flanking boats to stay on station in case of another attack. I beached the center boat and walked toward the compound, M-16 at the ready just in case. There was movement inside the perimeter, and I spotted Dai Ui Chuk and two Vietnamese walking with Don around the perimeter and surveying the damage. Dead VC lay everywhere: on the wires and in the ditch surrounding the berm, all in various stages of death, some frozen like ballet dancers in mid-air. One Vietnamese trooper came around the side of the bunker escorting a badly wounded VC who looked no older than a high school kid. Chuk and three of his troopers ran out of the compound and toward the village, where smoke still poured from a line of wooden huts.

As we looked over the compound, counting the dead VC and recovering weapons, we looked up and saw Chuk walking slowly back from the village. In his arms he carried one of his daughters. Her blood covered his uniform trousers and shirt and as he approached, it was evident the young girl was dead. Chuk stood in the still-smoldering debris, the sun now bursting forth with the first rays of intense light, his eyes looking mournful yet strong. Don gently took the limp body from Chuk who looked neither angry nor sad, and put the young child on the grass. Then he covered her with a blanket handed to him by one of the sergeants.

"What about Phuong and the second daughter?" Don asked. Chuk shook his head.

"Both gone, Tiu Ta, direct mortar hit." He walked away to the treeline and stood staring at the river, no sign of emotion on his face. We learned a great deal from the Vietnamese about feelings and face. Though stoic, on the inside they hurt every bit as much as we did.

Chuk remained subdued for days, but soon returned to his aggressive self and actually became more and more daring in his actions, as if asking to be hit. He survived a series of his own vicious counterattacks against the Vietcong in his district. The following year, Chuk lost a leg in close combat against a local Vietcong. Prior to the final North Vietnamese offensive in 1975, Chuk, by then a colonel, lost his remaining leg in a helicopter crash. He continued to resist the communist forces and was last seen in a re-education camp in the delta following the takeover in 1975.

The attack on the Kien Van headquarters was the first in what seemed like a continuous blur of actions which took place over the next three months. We learned shortly after returning to Sa Dec that although the town had been hit, only scattered outposts had been overrun. To the southeast, Vinh Long was in a state of siege for a week as the ARVN, followed by the U.S. Ninth Division, fought to clear the streets of VC who had penetrated and occupied sections of the city.

Unknown to us at the time, the North Vietnamese, together with VC main force units, had overrun portions of My Tho, including the area where the Catholic church and school were located. The buildings across the street from the school were taken over as a temporary command post by the VC until the second brigade from the U.S. Ninth Division from Dong Tam, with the mobile riverine force, retook the town and re-established control for the South Vietnamese. Shortly after the retaking of the city we heard that the bodies of nearly fifty Vietnamese civilians had been found near the school in the northern part of My Tho.

When the action subsided around Sa Dec, one month after the opening of the Offensive, I took a boat to My Tho to visit River Section 532 and 531 personnel. I also wanted to see what I could do to find Lung, but no one knew any details since U.S. personnel had been isolated in various pockets around the city during the attack. I feared the worst.

*   *   *

The post-Tet months saw the most action as our PBR patrols assisted the local Ninth ARVN and the local Rf and Pf forces as they tried to secure the area. The Vietcong controlled most roads and canals until we mounted joint operations to dislodge them but as soon as night fell, the territory often reverted right back to VC control.

The river patrol force suffered its heaviest losses during this period as the unit undertook almost daily canal incursions to support local outposts which had been overrun, captured, or faced nightly attacks. On March 24, 1968, in the backwaters of another Y area located about twenty-five kilometers southeast of Sa Dec, the unit lost three of its best sailors.

*   *   *

I dropped the radio hand-set, the voice pleading for artillery support fading but still audible in the crackling background. "Chief," I shouted, "get the stand-by boats, two relief crews—hurry. I'll meet them at the pier."

The warm, sleepy, Sunday afternoon atmosphere at the Mekong river patrol base in Sa Dec was interrupted by shouting and the sound of a jeep engine. We had survived mortar attacks, shellings, and even several ground assaults during the long months since the Tet Offensive began. Crisis was not new. But this time it was one of our own boat patrols in trouble. It was serious, and we moved with increased speed and intent. Charlie could shoot up the Ninth ARVN Vietnamese Division Army compound, assault outposts, raid the air strip, or hit the U.S. Army advisors' compound and we would respond with timely reaction patrols and support. When our own boats were hit, it was family, and we automatically reacted with more purpose. Our closeness galvanized us even more when we took casualties. We had a reputation for taking care of our own.

I headed for the jeep, buckling my pistol belt and donning my helmet and flak vest as I ran. "Bob," I shouted to my executive officer, Lieutenant Bob Donovan, "call for Dustoff (medevac) and Seawolf gunships—give them the coordinates."

Bo'sun Queenan swung into the jeep at the compound gate, buttoning his utilities and gathering his ammunition. He threw in his M-16 and flak jacket as I squealed out of the compound and turned onto the dirt road leading through Sa Dec to the boat piers. "I hear they're hit bad, Boss," Queenan said. "The Y's never been safe."

The junction in question was a confluence of two canals fifteen kilometers south of the main river between Vinh Long and Sa Dec. It was a dangerous area which, although guarded by two South Vietnamese regional force outposts—built during the strategic hamlet phase of the War—was totally controlled by the Vietcong outside the wires of the strongholds.

"They were loaded with wounded Viets, women and kids; got hit pulling them out of the outpost that's been under attack for the last three nights," I explained. "The province chief and senior advisor were both on Prendergast's boat. I think they were hit, too."

We skidded into the pier area, now alive with the two boat crews pulling off the PBR gun covers, warming up the twin diesel engines, and charging the twin 50-caliber bow-mounted machine guns. I ran to Queenan's boat, jumped the gunwale, turned on the FM radio, and dialed in the frequency for our operation center. "Base, this is Jungle Juliett, we're on the way. Are Dustoff and Seawolves coming?"

Bob Donovan answered, "Both on the way, Skipper. Dustoff will be there in one-five minutes. Be careful, Ninth Division operations just told us there are several units of VC with B-40s still in the area—they've got the ruff-puffs pinned down near the Dustoff LZ," he continued. "Be advised one boat is sunk, repeat sunk, and no security on the canal banks. Recommend you don't go in there until we get gunships—Jungle Juliett do you roger?" I heard, but was busy switching channels to contact Proffer's patrol.

"Delta 23, Delta 23, over," I said into the hand set. "Delta 23, Delta 23, over." Nothing but crackle. "Delta 23, Delta 23, this is Jungle Juliett, what's your status, over?" Still nothing. We pushed off into the stream, passed under the bridge spanning the canal leading into Sa Dec, and roared off.

The two boats glided at full throttle to the far canal bank and into the shallow water to get the added speed by jumping onto "the step" as we called the planing that resulted from the higher speed. When in a real hurry, we ran the shallow but more dangerous route a few feet from the canal bank. Both PBRs generated white foam rooster-tails that broke over the river water as the jacuzzi pumps whined at maximum revolutions. "Threat on both sides!," I shouted above the engine noise as we began the sweeping turn into the wide canal heading south toward the Y. Reacting automatically, the forward twin 50-caliber was swung to port and the after, single-gun to starboard. The two-boat patrol I had sent with Petty Officer Proffer early that morning with the province chief, Colonel Toung, senior advisor Colonel Jim South, and a handful of local regional/

popular force troopers called Rf/Pfs, had gone down the canals to the outpost near the Y. Their mission was to evacuate the wounded and their families after three consecutive night attacks had nearly overrun their barbed-wire outpost. Colonel South had called me in on Saturday afternoon to show me the relief plan, which called for one company of Rfs to work their way down the east side of the canal giving one bank security for the two boats of Proffer's patrol to bring in Colonel Toung and evacuate the survivors.

As we neared the area, I noticed how high the canal banks were above us. The water was very low due to the season and the moon phase. Surprisingly, even this far from the Mekong mouth, the effects of the South China Sea tides were substantial. This was not a good position for the boats, I thought, again regretting sending the patrol out under these conditions. Our advantages of speed and mobile firepower were minimized by the low water conditions. I should have insisted on helicopter gunship escort before going in, but it was hard to say no when there were wounded to evacuate. As the only all-American unit in the province, I made the extra effort to be aggressive and to try to set an example for the local Vietnamese forces, which were not noted for their enthusiasm to find a fight.

Queenan, the keen-eyed first class bo'sun mate from Brooklyn and two-year veteran of fighting on the Mekong, noticed the unusual height of both canal banks. He looked at me and shook his head. "Water's too damn low, Boss. This is how it was when I got hit here a year ago." Queenan had been wounded the first of three times in this same location a year earlier when he was a boat coxswain. For that action, he was awarded the Silver Star for heroism supporting local forces.

We passed under a badly damaged bridge, rounded a bend in the canal, and heard the sounds of a helicopter lifting off. The cloud of brown dust and flying debris stirred up by the huge blades was just beginning to settle. The medevac helo had just left the scene. There was no sound of gunfire anymore, only the sounds of our engines as we saw the helo gain altitude and turn northeast toward Dong Tam and the Ninth U.S. Division Field Hospital near My Tho. I watched it swing in a wide arc toward the main river and wondered how many of our sailors were aboard and how badly they were hurt. I knew there were several wounded judging from the screams I heard over the radio as the ambush first erupted.

Queenan's shout broke my thoughts. "Sir, there's one!," he yelled as he pointed ahead. On the right bank of the canal was one of our boats, beached, with engines still running slowly to keep her bow on the bank. There was no one aboard and I thought, they must all be on the helo. Inside the boat there were only the dead.

It was a scene of utter carnage. First Class Petty Officer Proffer, the patrol officer, lay dead on the engine covers, his right leg shattered from the knee down and a dark bruise on his head. In the stern, around the base of the after 50-caliber mount, lay what was left of the young gunner. Apparently he had been hit by a B-40 rocket directly in the stomach. There was nothing recognizable about him.

I resisted the urge to vomit, and turned to the radio, which somehow remained intact, just as a hail of bullets snapped overhead, several pinging against the cockpit armor. As I turned instinctively toward the sound, I heard Queenan shout, "Rocket to port, get down!" I saw it arching in the air with the black smoke trail coming from the far bank. I suddenly remembered that we couldn't maneuver—we were still on the beach. I closed my eyes and hunkered down. This is it, I thought. The rocket hit the treeline behind us with a *wump* and Queenan's 50-calibers and M-16s began pouring fire into the VC rocket position. I jumped back into Queenan's boat and we raced deeper into the canal toward the outpost.

"Base, this is Jungle Juliett. Bob, send two more PBRs and the mike boat with a volunteer crew as fast as possible. We're still getting fire but we're going after our boat."

"Roger, Juliett," Lieutenant Bob Donovan replied. "I can hear the background. Hang in there, Skipper, we're comin' with more boats."

Queenan and the other boat crew continued to return fire into the treeline. All I could think about was the second PBR located somewhere downstream. We had to recover the boat and her crew. There was enough daylight left to go further downstream to retrieve the second PBR, which according to the Rf soldiers loitering around the beached boat when we arrived, was floating bow up. I knew from their description that the PBR was either capsized or holed. There was so much styrofoam in the bow they never sank completely, even with the weight of the on-board weapons. We had to at least retrieve the 50-calibers: the local area would be a disaster if the VC got their hands on those weapons. Thoughts of recovering those weapons and our crews gnawed at me and drove me on. I was determined to find that boat.

As we waited for the mike boat, Donovan arranged with the Ninth Division for an escort of Cobra gunship helicopters to cover us as we started downstream again. While we waited in the heat, two figures suddenly bolted from the tall grass across the canal, running like gazelles toward the water.

"Hey, they're ours, Sir. They must'a swam for it," Queenan shouted. "Over here!," he called, just as a dozen shots rang out from across the canal. I watched as the two survivors jumped through the grass followed by two figures in green sun helmets. Time seemed to stand still. The sun blazed wildly and all movement seemed exaggerated and deliberate. A high-pitched screech filled the air, and a shrill sound I did not recognize added to the din. I suddenly realized it was my own voice that I heard.

"Get in the water!," I was yelling, and the two sailors dove onto their bellies and crawled the remaining few yards through the muddy canal bank. In desperation, I raised my Colt .45 automatic and emptied it into the hopelessly out-of-range shoreline. As the two sailors hit the water, as if on signal, Queenan and the forward gunner opened fire into the high grass. When we saw both the surviving crewmen safely in the canal, we opened up with everything we had, including our M-79 grenade launchers. The sun helmets disappeared in the dust and flying coconut grass. The forward gunner of the second boat, now about fifty yards behind us, swung the double-50 mount around to port and opened fire, blasting the tops off the high grass with a deadly spray of tracer-laced fire. The clatter and loud popping of the two forward 50s made me shudder. No one could possibly survive in front of that barrage. It was frightening even to be behind the mount as the hot spent rounds cluttered the deck. The smell of burning cordite seared our nostrils as dirt and dust flew around the boat.

The fire from across the canal stopped after a few final rounds hit against the thin armor plating around the coxswain's cockpit. We helped the two relieved crewmen out of the muddy water into our boat, shoved them into the enclosed forward compartment, and wrapped them in blankets. While the boats circled, waiting for the other boats and gunships, we heard the full story of what had happened from the two survivors.

The lead boat had pulled away from the outpost, carrying Colonels Toung and South. There were about fifteen wounded Vietnamese, including women and children, crammed on the boat, sitting on the engine covers, the gunwales, the canopy, and behind the gunners. The second boat followed in trail similarly loaded, unable to move faster than several knots. Both were heading north toward the safety of the main river when all hell broke loose. The lead boat had taken at least one B-40 that killed the rear gunner. Heavy machine gun fire from across the canal had killed the patrol officer, Petty Officer Proffer, and wounded Coxswain Prendergast. Colonels Toung and South and an unknown number of the fleeing Viets had returned fire.

The second boat, from which the two survivors had escaped, received one rocket round in the bow just at the waterline, causing the boat to lurch and capsize with the heavy load of extra passengers. They all fell into the water in a mass of swirling mud, bundles, and debris. The crew attempted to swim clear of the boat, but the canal was only waist deep and they could only crawl through the slime and muck toward the far bank. The two crew members somehow made it to the east bank, where they had first hidden and then quietly worked their way north toward the bridge at the bend and the medevac helicopter, which had landed nearby. The third crewman, Petty Officer Henderson, had reached the west bank, opposite the VC, and had managed to run the entire way to the bridge in time to board the helicopter and help the wounded from the first boat make their escape.

We had to re-enter that cauldron to get the boat. As we waited in the afternoon heat, the mosquitos swarmed, and the smell of fish sauce hung in the air. The atmosphere seemed heavy with anticipation and the smell of blood and the dead. The knot of onlookers melted away, and only a handful of regional force troops, barefoot in their black pajama bottoms, stood around lazily edging closer and closer to the beached boat. Queenan turned and lobbed a concussion grenade into the water near the soldiers. "The bastards," he muttered. "They're going for the stuff in the boat. Next one that touches the boat gets a slug through his hand." I tried to calm him but, he had seen a lot, and maybe three times wounded was too much for one man. But he was still the best. The Vietnamese local forces lived and fought on a shoestring. They would steal anything not tied down, but it was a sad case when all they wanted were grenades and ammo from our shot-up boat. So many things in this war did not make sense.

At last we heard the engines of the approaching twin diesel mike boat, officially designated an LCM (Landing Craft Medium). This craft had been specially configured for long river operations, and could carry a large 1500-gallon fuel bladder, spare ammunition, and rations. It also had two 50-caliber machine guns mounted in the bow and a 60-millimeter mortar in a sand-box to absorb the shock in the well deck. We needed this World War II relic with its powerful engines to tow out the sunken PBR. It could be run aground and refloated, was tough, seaworthy, and was made of steel. The coxswain position was exposed on the stern, protected only by a quarter-inch steel plate—not much good against the deadly B-40 rockets, which could penetrate even thicker armor.

Donovan had assembled a group of volunteers armed with a mix of M-16s, the navy M-14s, and the deadly M-79 grenade launchers. Two additional PBRs escorted the mike boat, with Chief Quartermaster Simmons as the patrol officer. The Cobra gunships from the Ninth U.S. Division checked in and circled overhead, awaiting our departure. I rode on the stern of the mike boat, next to a large heavy-duty cleat and a long coil of one-inch manila line that lay at my feet. We had to get the stern of the mike boat in close enough to the exposed bow of the sunken PBR to tie onto a towing pad-eye on the strong point in the bow, the only part of the boat strong enough to take the force of a tow—if that was possible with the boat full of water. I had never tried it before, but it was the only way.

We pushed off behind two PBRs led by Queenan, with me on a radio behind the coxswain, and eleven riflemen and grenade launchers arrayed against the starboard side, which was the west side of the canal and the source of the initial hostile fire. An additional two PBRs followed, with their heavy 50-caliber guns trained on both canal banks. The Cobra gunships could provide fire suppression simultaneously onto both sides of the canal. Our speed was limited by the lumbering mike boat, and there was not sufficient water in the canal for the PBRs to orbit around her. They were thus even more vulnerable targets, moving on a straight and slow path.

We commenced intermittent harassing fire against the west bank of the canal. The hamlets on the east bank were still manned by friendly troops. All went well for the first five kilometers as we slowly passed the first outpost. The local forces stood on the tops of their berm and cheered us as we inched by. After another hundred meters, the canal narrowed and took a sharp turn to the right. Around the bend was the location of the ambush. The second compound was situated to the left, on the east bank.

We came to the bend and rounded it just as Queenan called on the radio, "Got the boat in sight. Her bowline's tied to a tree just beyond the outpost on the opposite bank." That made it even more difficult, since we would have to position the exposed stern of the mike boat against the west bank to connect the towline. Queenan started firing short bursts of M-16 and occasionally 50-caliber rounds into the heavily wooded high bank. The bank lay a good ten feet above the waterline, which meant the 50-caliber guns had to be elevated considerably. There was little chance for sweeping ground fire since the rounds just cut the edge of the bank and rose skyward, leaving red tracer trails above the rice paddies farther inland.

As the landing craft rounded the bend, I saw Major Anderson, the district advisor, waving from the small observation tower of the outpost. He was a brave man who had spent two of the last three harrowing nights in the outpost assisting the local forces. With an American advisor on the scene, our patrols got straight information. The major had functioned as an on-site spotter for the gunships and PBRs. So far we received no fire as we groped our way downstream in the narrow canal. The four PBRs took protecting positions against the two banks, and we backed the mike boat against the canal edge where the tip of the sunken PBR bow was just visible, still tied to a tree. As we neared the bow, I climbed out onto the stern sheets of the mike boat and leaned out with the bitter end of the towline in my hands. I could just reach the bow, but could not get the towline into the towing eye without first removing the line tied to the tree. If I cut the bowline, the PBR would lurch downstream and we would have to chase it. I felt my performance was a circus act, with my exposed rear end flapping in the breeze. I had no protection from the heavy underbrush of the canal bank just a few yards away. I tried to figure out how to hook securely onto the bowline amidst the gunfire surrounding me.

I was amazed by what came to mind, with my thoughts on a hundred details and frightened stiff. I remembered the ancient chief petty officer instructor in Annapolis during plebe summer taking great pains to show a group of totally disinterested fourth-classmen the finer points of tying a bowline or sheep-shank knot in the Dahlgren Hall sail loft jack-stay. There had been such wisdom and purpose in everything done at the Naval Academy. And now only the simple act of knot-tying stood between success and possible failure. It renewed my deep respect for those who had in their wisdom subjected us to those basic skills.

I quickly tied a bowline followed by a sheep-shank in the line holding the PBR to the tree, shouted to the coxswain to go ahead at full power, and stood ready to cut the tree side with a sharp kaybar knife. As I hung onto the stern of the mike boat, I heard the encouraging sounds of bursts of fire designed to keep unwanted heads down on the canal bank. Suddenly I realized that some of those rounds were ricochetting off the sides of the boat near my feet. My God, that fire was coming from inside the trees! Praying that the towline would hold, I slithered to the inboard side of the coxswain's platform, where I looked up at the flag flying from the staff above the coxswain shelter not two feet from both our heads. It hung like a piece of shredded lace, torn to bits by the incoming gunfire directed at the two of us on the stern.

We slowly extracted, with the gunships making repeated firing runs to suppress the light fire coming at us from the high banks. The knots held and we churned north, slowly emerging from the confusion of sound. Each foot we progressed north brought greater relief. When we neared the spot where we had found our first boat beached, we secured the sunken unit to the bridge. The worst part of the operation was the aftermath, when the elation of having made it through gave way to disgust when we found the body of a small boy wedged between the engine cover and one engine, having been stuck there, submerged since the ambush that morning.

* * *

One aspect of small unit command in Vietnam which called for detailed planning, imagination, and not a little excitement was SEAL operations. As commanders of designated stretches of the Mekong and the adjacent canals, the PBR river section commanders frequently had SEAL teams assigned under their operational control. These highly trained and unique special warfare units usually operated as independent platoons. Although they came under our task organization, they worked independently.

SEAL teams were usually assigned in Vietnam on six-month tours and moved often from one area to another. As a result, they did not share the same intimate knowledge of the river and canals as the PBR river sailors, who operated in the same areas for one or even two years and spent many hours on patrols. Consequently, the transient SEAL teams that shared our accommodations, pier areas, and logistic support drew heavily on the PBR sailors' detailed knowledge of the waters. This was the case when I operated in both My Tho and Sa Dec.

SEAL operations were based on perishable intelligence and therefore, as quick-reaction forces, often counted on the PBRs to insert them on their night reconnaissance missions, ambushes, and listening posts. We liked the joint operations with the SEALs that targeted VC areas which had given the PBRs difficulty during patrols and those where the operations supported friendly local villages. The SEALs were trained in small unit tactics ashore and they complimented our waterborne fighting capabilities nicely. Some of our more successful missions with them resulted in large numbers of Vietcong killed and captured in Dinh Tuong and Ham Luong Provinces in 1967, especially around Tan Toi and Devil's Island. Later in Sa Dec, our river section operated with SEALs in all the provinces from Sa Dec to the Cambodian border.

In Sa Dec during the post-Tet period, I was asked one day by the senior American province advisor, a civilian named Jim Smith, if my river section would consider cooperating with the CIA Phoenix program. I had complete operational autonomy and could operate our PBRs with whatever allied units I chose. In my unbridled enthusiasm and naïveté, I did not ask many questions, but eagerly offered my assistance.

Phoenix was the CIA program designed to undermine the Vietcong infrastructure by turning their own tactics against them. The name Phoenix was a rough translation of phung hoang, a mythical Vietnamese bird endowed with certain omnipotent attributes. The objective was to neutralize the Vietcong's National Liberation Front (NLF) by using former Vietcong who had defected or could be hired to turn against their own. To carry out this mission, Paramilitary Reconnaissance Units (PRUs) were organized and trained by U.S. Special Operations personnel to capture or otherwise eliminate the VC support.

At the time I knew only that they needed reliable riverborne transport to take special Phoenix units to certain positions at night and to provide heavy machine gun support from the river and canals as necessary, especially during the vulnerable extraction following an operation. The PRUs used for the Sa Dec based operations were led by Americans, either Army Special Forces or Navy SEALs. I was told by the local CIA sector advisors that the PRUs consisted mostly of re-trained Chu Hois, Vietcong defectors from the local areas where they would operate.

The concept was sound, and at the time we were weary and disgusted with tactics used by the local Vietcong, who had been particularly active in our area prior to and immediately following the

Tet Offensive. I had personally been in villages immediately following VC night terror raids and had helped the local villagers clean up the mutilated and often decapitated bodies of school teachers and local leaders who had been selectively eliminated in the VC's program of terror. The Phoenix program, if carried out precisely, seemed like the perfect counter to those tactics. My section participated and I went as patrol leader on the first operation, which commenced near midnight several nights later.

I met with the American leader of the planned strike. He was a Navy SEAL, first class petty officer. I was impressed by his sharp mind, physical condition, and apparent grasp of operational planning. However, he knew little of the local area where he would take his PRU on the first operation. As a result, he was keen to use boats with crews that knew the area well and could operate effectively at night.

The operation consisted of a late night insertion on a canal entrance we knew well. The small force was to proceed to an objective which was a permanent VC base. It was to enter, guided by the precise experience of a former operative from that camp. I was told the plan was to abduct two particular leaders for intelligence exploitation. The SEAL leader, Mike, did not tell me the specifics of the operation, nor did I ask. My job was to get the team to their launch point and to pick them up at one of several designated points before first light. In between those tasks, we were to stand off in the main river with the boats some distance upstream, drift, and wait for radio signal which would indicate which extraction point to use.

We arrived at a designated pick-up point far from our regular base area to embark the PRU. As we waited with the PBR bows beached on the riverbank, I began to think the PRUs were either expertly concealing their departure point, or something had gone wrong. Thirty minutes later I saw a dark figure emerge from the treeline. It was Mike, "My PRUs are a little late Sir. Are you ready?"

"We've been here since the designated time," I answered, impressed by the stealth his team showed as a dozen Vietnamese appeared by our boats, as if from nowhere. They were all in black pajamas, had camouflaged faces, and wore red bandannas around their heads or necks. They were lightly armed with close-range automatic weapons and knives. They divided up as planned and quickly but silently boarded the three PBRs. Mike boarded my boat. When we reached the main river, I asked him how these men were compensated. He looked at me in the dark and whispered, "Oh, we pay them a bounty for each VC they kill or bring back alive." I said nothing, but wondered how the mechanics of that system worked. I learned later that night.

All went as planned, and we reached a point several hundred meters upstream from the insertion spot, cut engines, and drifted into the shoreline one boat at a time while the others drifted offshore as security. We disembarked the PRUs, and drifted off downstream into the center of the main river. After waiting an hour, we powered about five kilometers upstream, cut engines, and settled down to await the pick-up signal. The night was particularly dark and still. Sound on nights like that carried far on the river.

About one hour later a great firefight broke out, apparently in an area several kilometers from where we had disembarked the team. As I studied the approximate map coordinates of the flashes and sound of fire with a small, red-lensed flashlight, I realized that whatever was taking place was at or very near a popular friendly force outpost. We saw tracers arching high into the night sky. There were short bursts of automatic weapons and the occasional *wump* of a grenade. We sat and listened, wondering what was happening, and waited for the pre-arranged signal, but nothing came. Silence came and still we waited.

Two hours after the firing had ceased, I heard the designated number of clicks on the frequency which gave the extraction point. We proceeded downstream again at low speed and cut engines before drifting ashore one at a time. We saw the infrared signal and waited for the PRUs to come out. They came, two less than had been inserted and two bleeding from slight wounds. Mike joined us as we shoved off. There were no prisoners.

As we started engines again and began our run back to their base area, I noticed something wet against my arm. The boat was more crowded than usual with the added passengers. One of the PRU members was pushed close to me. I looked down, and was able to see blood. Thinking one more man was wounded, I tapped Mike and pointed to the blood on my hand which had come from what appeared to be a nasty open wound on the man's side. Mike just grinned and shook his head, "Don't worry, Sir, that's not his blood." More curious, I looked again and turned on my small red map light. Tied on a string around the man's waist were three human ears dripping semi-clotted blood onto the deck.

The team disembarked in silence at their base area. I said nothing more to Mike, thinking they must have achieved their objective, only without their prisoners. When I got back to my small operations center, Bob Donovan saw me, "Boss, call Major Anderson over at sub-sector headquarters. Better call now, he seems real upset."

Instead of calling, I jumped into my jeep and drove over to the headquarters. I felt the tired calm I always felt after an all-night patrol, and looked forward to the bacon, eggs, and coffee served at the sub-sector compound. I drove through the barbed-wire gate, past the sleepy Vietnamese sentry, his carbine dangling carelessly from his hands. Inside I met Major Anderson. He was looking tired and drawn. His puffy eyes indicated he had not slept the whole night either. We sat down together over coffee.

"What the hell happened last night, Peter?" he asked, trying to conceal that he was upset. Major Anderson was a prince of an officer. He was an ROTC infantry officer from Duke and highly respected as one of the most dedicated advisors. He spent most of his time out with his local force troops showing them how things were done and, with his small American staff, had been in many skirmishes while giving the Vietnamese support. He had initiated solid programs among his local forces, which were beginning to pay off. This was his second tour as an advisor in Vietnam.

"What do you mean?" I asked, anticipating what was going to come.

"Didn't you have a patrol out last night near Ap Phu Dinh outpost?" That was the name of the post near where we had inserted the PRUs.

"Yes Sir," I said. "We were on a special op with PRUs. Why?" The Major was not supposed to know about the exact objective of the PRU operation, even though it was near one of his outposts. At least I was not supposed to be the one to tell him. I was surprised he had not already been briefed by the CIA people.

"Cut the 'Sir' shit, Pete. Some bastards ran into one of Phu Dinh's security patrols outside the outpost, waxed them, and then attacked the outpost itself."

"It couldn't have been the PRUs we were carrying. They were going to a specific VC target," I said.

"Well, whoever it was killed three of my best Rfs at Phu Dinh and mutilated the bodies. Can you believe they cut off their goddamn ears," the major exclaimed. "If your operation was in the same area, at the same time, how the hell could the VC have done that?"

My mind was racing. Why didn't Mike say anything to me about running into friendlies? He must have known if his PRUs fired into the outpost. "Look, I'll find out more about this."

I left and drove to the CIA base near the sector compound. I walked into the main reception room and there was Mike, talking with one of the senior CIA advisors. "What the hell happened last night at Ap Phu Dinh?" I asked. They both looked at me and began to laugh.

"Well, it looks like some of our guys got a little carried away last night," the advisor said. I had seen him several times but did not know his name. He was a man of medium build, with a pockmarked face and sizable paunch. He did not look like a man who was in the field very often. I knew he was a former army officer from Special Forces and on loan to the agency. I had heard him speak fluent Vietnamese. I tried not to ask too many questions when in their compound.

There was a second man, soft-spoken and congenial. His name was Jake. I had spoken to him several times at the advisors' club on the Ninth ARVN American advisors' compound. He spoke so softly he was often hard to hear.

"They ran into some security from the Rf/Pf outpost at Phu Duc and ended up exchanging a shot or two," said the advisor.

"Then they hit the outpost," I injected.

"Well," they laughed. "These guys are used to hitting outposts. Can't win 'em all." I watched astounded, as they continued to joke about the operation. Several other Americans entered the room.

One asked, "Were you out with our team last night?"

Mike answered for me. "Yeah, Sid, the lieutenant here is the PBR section commander. He put us in and picked us up last night."

Sid, a small yet strongly-built man, looked pleased. "Well, your boys did an excellent job last night getting our team in and out. Mike said he was very impressed with your troops' professionalism." I suspected I was being complimented to calm me down.

Mike added, "They were superb, Lieutenant. We'd like to work with you on a regular basis."

I was confused. "Was your part successful? I thought you got hit on the way to the base camp," I said, pretending I had not seen the ears. "I thought the mission had been aborted after your contact."

"No, we didn't quite get what we wanted, but our guys got a taste of blood and they're ready to hit the same place again," Jake said quietly.

"We heard about the Ap Phu Dinh outpost. Too bad, but it's no big thing. The PRUs got some kills and will be ready to go out again soon," Sid said.

"Have you heard what happened at the outpost?" I asked, beginning to lose the edge. I was tired and aggravated.

"Yeah, there was a mix up, and I guess one of the PRUs has a personal grudge with some of the Rfs there. They walked into their outer perimeter patrol and took some hits. The outer patrol is new, never used to have it. Caught our guys off guard. Usually you could pass the place without even waking them up. They're lazy bastards, used to sleep all the time," Sid replied.

I knew Major Anderson had just forced all his outposts to conduct outer perimeter patrols as an active measure to preempt VC probes and sneak attacks. He was immensely proud that they were continuing the procedure, especially since the Tet period, when they were hit so often. They managed to keep from being overrun by preempting several sapper and large main-force attacks. Now this.

"Sir, didn't you report the contact with the outpost to the subsector advisor, Major Anderson? He'll want to know about it, especially if some of his men were killed," I was becoming irritated with the conversation.

"Shit no," said Sid, who was apparently very senior. The others showed a little deference in the way they stood in front of him. The CIA official continued, "They're riddled with informers over there. I don't want them discussing our ops. We keep these on a strict, need-to-know basis. I know he's your buddy, Peter, but I don't want you discussing this with him. Our work with you is not for dissemination."

I had not sent in an after-action report myself, since my boats had not been engaged in hostile fire exchange. We did not report routine operations with local forces unless we expended ammunition and took hits or made kills. I had been told by the sector senior advisor that I could not report the operations with the PRUs, but I had not decided what to do if we made contact or took hits. I would have been required to report. I had planned to log the operation as "local ops in support of friendly ground forces." I disliked what I was hearing.

"What happened to your two PRUs who didn't come back to the pick-up point?" I asked. "We only brought ten out."

"Don't worry, Peter, they're all right," Jake said. He put his hand on my shoulder, seeing I was getting testy. "I heard we hit some Viets in the outpost."

"You sure did," I said, blurting out what I had heard from Major Anderson. "You sure as hell did. Your wonderful PRUs killed three of Anderson's troopers." I was getting angrier. "Your PRUs not only hit the outer perimeter security patrol Major Anderson had sent out, but attacked the goddamn outpost, and wounded a couple civilians. What the hell were the PRUs doing?" The whole scene did not make sense now that it was coming out.

"Sir," I said, turning to Sid. "We inserted your team with Mike in charge as arranged, and picked them up on signal. Your people came back acting like they won a fight, and all they did was hit a friendly outpost! How the hell can you justify that?"

"Calm down, Lieutenant," he said. "We're the overall coordinators for this operation delta-wide. It's just getting started, and the most important thing is that our PRUs gain confidence in each other and in us. They have to know we're not going to back out on them and we'll reward them for tough duty. Otherwise they're liable to go back to the other side."

I could not believe my ears. "You mean you're going to reward them for what happened last night? They killed friendlies plus hit some civilians, and you're going to pay them?" I was beginning to think this was a bad dream. I had not mentioned the ears hanging around the Chu Hoi's waist, but now I blurted it out. "You mean to tell me you're going to pay those bastards for bringing back trophies proving they killed friendlies?" I was shouting.

The senior advisor took me by the arm. "Settle down Pete. You've been up all night. You'll feel better after some rest."

"You've got to look at the big picture," he continued. "We've got to build these teams up to where they're really effective. They're the only ones who can lead us back to their own units so we can use their own tactics on Charlie." He started pacing like a coach addressing a football team in a locker room. "To gain their loyalty we have to break a few eggs. We can't afford to cry over a little spilt milk." He emphasized the word break with his fist in his hand. "You've seen the mess Charlie leaves in the villages. The only way we can get back at them is by using their own tactics." He began to lecture in a big leadership voice, and his face puffed up. "Peter, you've been here damn near a year, you know what a mess it is. Now, for the first time, we have carte blanche to use their own medicine and kick ass. Now the last thing we need is to get soft and ruin this area for the future. I'll speak to Jim Smith. He thinks highly of you and your PBR sailors and wants to work together. Now go get some rest. We'll talk about this later."

He steered me gently toward the door, whispering to me in a low voice. "Now I don't want any written reports on this operation. That's our job."

I left the compound, disgusted, got in my jeep, and drove back to my compound. I was tired and shaken but could not sleep. That evening, I wrote out a message report of the patrol the night before, laying out exactly what happened. I added as a last paragraph the following:

"Unodir (unless otherwise directed) I will not permit further participation by River Patrol Section 513 in operations in support of the PRU in conjunction with Phoenix." I sent the message to the Navy River Patrol Headquarters in Canh Tho, CTF 116. I never received an answer.

I left Vietnam on April 5, 1968, several weeks later, after being directed to move my section out of Sa Dec down to the headquarters of Canh Tho. It was a routine move, I was told.

At a short change of command ceremony with only my troops present, I introduced my replacement. I gave a brief farewell talk praising my men for their good work and reminding them to keep a sense of compassion while on the river. I was surprised when Bo'sun Queenan stepped forward, and on behalf of the section, presented me with a gold watch. It could not have come from a finer petty officer.

The results of the Phoenix program are a matter of history. According to results published by Mr. William Colby, who ran the Phoenix program in 1968, more than 20,000 Vietnamese were killed in this operation and an additional 28,000 captured. According to the communist leaders, the cumulative effects of the Tet Offensive and Phoenix cost the NLF their best leaders and rendered them nearly ineffective. This was borne out by the fact that the Vietcong units were not utilized during the final two major North Vietnamese offensives, in 1972 and finally in 1975, when they reached their goal of overrunning South Vietnam.

There have been debates concerning the use of the terms "assassination" versus "killed" or "neutralized" in conjunction with the Phoenix operation. The episode above indicates the futility of trying to establish hard fact when accounting for the detailed results of that effort.

Chapter VI
Survival

Lung

Life in our village during the weeks following the escape from the fighting in My Tho became more and more difficult. The Vietcong visited us more often and demanded to be lodged in our homes. As a result, many villagers left and sought safer places closer to the government outposts. But some could not afford relocation. Moving closer to the protected hamlets also exposed the families to the dangers of armed attack. The choice was between an uncertain existence and assured terror and attack.

Nights in the village became intolerable. Airplanes began to bomb the Phu Duc area after visits by the Vietcong. We could not stay in the houses at night and were forced to sleep in the fields. We were often scared, and the lack of regular sleep compounded our misery. We wished for the peaceful days of the past.

One night, while running into the fields for shelter, my youngest brother was killed by falling bombs. He was only eight years old. It was monsoon season, wet and cold. We had been running after the first alarm of air attack. He fell behind with the noise and disappeared into a cloud of smoke and debris. We were knocked down in the mud by the blast. The force of the wind following the flash of light seemed to suck the air out of our lungs. Dazed and shaken, each of us recovered, located Mother, and looked for a place to hide. Suddenly, I saw my brother lying face down in the mud. I shrieked at him to get up, but he did not move. The steady rain washed away the mud that had fallen on his back. I thought of the water buffalo, and how they loved the thick mud of this season. The buffalo always rose from the mud just when you thought they had disappeared. But my little brother lay in the mud and never rose again.

To make matters worse, during one of the many daytime searches conducted by the South Vietnamese foot-soldiers, my oldest brother was arrested, accused of being a Vietcong, and taken away. The situation became very difficult for my mother, since there were only three sons left to work, and I was a burden because of my leg. The war and the frequent presence of the Vietcong in the village made life unbearable.

Two months had passed since Tet when I had fled the school in My Tho. I heard that things had grown better there and that the Vietcong had left again. At least there was less bombing in My Tho, and no nightly visits by the guerrilla fighters seeking shelter. But space to live in My Tho was limited. Nevertheless, I would be less a burden there, so I decided to return.

The water taxi was the same as the one I had taken with Din many months before. It was curious to remember the thrill and apprehension before the first trip. Din and I had anticipated stepping out into the world by crossing the river for the first time. By the time I left the village after Tet, I had made the dangerous crossing many times, often alone.

The embankment in My Tho stood high and crowded, still a formidable obstacle for me and my leg. But the scramble up its steep side was rewarded by a stroll through the park and the long walk up the wide My Tho Boulevard to my school. Although there was still damage visible, life appeared to have returned to normal. There were many South Vietnamese and American soldiers in the streets. As I approached the school, the vision of my last night there came to mind. I recalled the vivid picture of the Vietcong soldier as he ran out into the very street I was walking on and was cut down by the tank.

The school still showed some damage. The sisters had fixed much of the collapsed roof and swept away the broken planters and splintered tiles. School was again in session. I went into the courtyard where sister Phuong had fallen, and I imagined the spot still carried a mark of her blood. There was an unreal feeling, as if revisiting a dream.

One of the sisters recognized me and took me into the cool room off the terrace where the sisters sometimes gathered for tea. After talking with them, it was understood that I could not return to the school. There was no money to pay the tuition. The American sailors had not come by since I had left.

I walked down the busy road back to the Victory Hotel to look for Trung Shi Davis. The Americans were still there, and the guards recognized me and let me in. But the place looked different; it was completely surrounded now by sandbags and barbed-wire. Trung Shi Davis was no longer there. The sailors looked nervous and were not very friendly. The office with the big 532 sign on it was full of new sailors, so I chose not to go in.

I stood around for awhile and finally spotted Minh, of the river police. He greeted me but was abrupt, and like the sailors, he was nervous.

He told me that there had been some things stolen from the sailors' office where Dai Ui Peter's replacement was, and the Americans were blaming the loss on the Vietnamese helpers.

"Where is Co Thuong?" I asked. Minh looked at me crossly.

"Don't mention her name here. The Americans believe she was a Vietcong spy."

"Where is she?" I whispered.

"I don't know. She never came back after the attacks during Tet." Minh looked around nervously. "For all I know, she may have been killed. Anyway, she's never been back. If they hear you talk about her, they'll get mean and ask you lots of questions."

"Where's Mr. Phu from the army compound?"

"He was killed during Tet—died leading a group of Vietcong armed with explosives into the army advisors' camp," Minh snapped. "Better run along, Lung. It's not the same here now. The Americans don't trust anyone, not even us."

I thought it best if I left before they suspected me of stealing. I quickly departed the compound and never went back. My heart was sad, not so much because I could not continue the school, but because of the bad feelings that had grown between the Americans and the Vietnamese. Most of all I was sad that Trung Shi Davis was gone. I hoped that he had not been hurt, or worse.

During the next days, I stayed with my cousin's family in My Tho. Life was difficult for them too, and I finally decided to go to the Rehabilitation Center where Co Yen was, to see if she could help me. I got a ride on a bus which stopped several times because of roadblocks. As I sat in the crowded, hot bus, I remembered my first trip to Saigon in the jeep with Sergeant Dinh, Dai Ui Peter, and Trung Shi Davis. I thought of how happy we had been after reaching the hospital, how we all laughed and pretended there had been no danger.

On the outskirts of Saigon, soldiers stopped the bus and searched us all. They were looking for Vietcong in the bus. I had heard there was frequent fighting in the streets of Saigon.

I finally reached the center and found Co Yen. She was kind as always and listened to my story. I asked Yen if it were possible to work in the hospital as I knew they trained handicapped there. Yen said I was still too young for training. She sent me instead to Me Linh Center in Saigon. This was a home sponsored by a women's organization under the guidance of Mrs. Thieu, the wife of the President of South Vietnam. It was a center formed to support handicapped children. They happily accepted me, and I remained there for two years. The time went by slowly, but it was relatively quiet and I learned many skills.

After months of trying, I was able to get into a career training center for handicapped young people, so I could learn to support myself. I was accepted into a Catholic church on Tu Xuong Street, where the nuns taught me how to sew and embroider. After school hours, I did chores in the church, cleaning and carrying water. I was able to work and study in this fashion. Life seemed settled for me, and I enjoyed the quiet of the church and the gentle sisters. I heard from my mother often.

In 1972, when I was fifteen, my brother was released from prison, but was required to serve in the Army of the Republic of Vietnam. The next year he was killed in battle. With the loss of her second oldest son, things became close to unbearable for my mother. I decided to return to My Tho where I could work and bring my earnings to her. I lived in My Tho with my cousin, where I did chores and sewed and embroidered for a tailor.

I was able to live in the relatively quiet surroundings of My Tho at the home of my cousin until 1975, when the communists took over Saigon and the rest of South Vietnam. It was a beautiful day in April when the first North Vietnamese soldiers came into My Tho. I remember it well.

I was walking back from the market, carrying several baskets of pineapple and mangoes I had not managed to sell. I heard a loud roar on the main road. People began to gather along the boulevard to watch. I walked alone up the main street and soon came to the old Victory Hotel.

The Americans had long since gone, and the hotel was being used by the South Vietnamese sailors to whom the Americans had given their river boats before they left. The sign painted on the hotel entrance was of two flags, the American red, white, and blue entwined with the red and yellow of the Republic of South Vietnam. I stood quietly and looked at the spot by the sandbagged guard post, under the large weeping tree, as Trung Shi Davis called it. That was where Dai Ui Peter, Roderick Davis, and I always met to go to the market or for walks and rides in the jeep. The tree was still there; only one large branch had been broken during the street fighting of Tet in 1968. The place where the branch had been broken off was covered by a large scar. I always looked at the scar on that tree when I went by the Victory Hotel, for somehow it reminded me of my leg and how both the tree and my body grew similar scar tissue to hide the wounds.

I saw dust on the road coming from the north. I stopped across from the hotel and watched as a long line of trucks approached. They were full of soldiers wearing brown and green helmets who carried flags of red and blue with a large yellow star in the center. I had seen that flag before, when the Vietcong came to the village, and as it hung in hamlets which had been attacked at night and then abandoned. The Vietcong left the flags as a sign that they had been there. As a child I had always thought the Vietcong had not liked their own flag and for that reason kept trying to lose it or leave it all over the countryside.

The trucks rolled by, but no one cheered or made any noise; they just looked in curiosity. Then the line stopped. The truck nearest me was full of soldiers. They looked bored and tired. After they had been stopped for some time, one of the soldiers noticed the sign hanging above the Victory Hotel entrance. He pointed to it, and a group of the soldiers began shooting their assault guns at it from the truck. Then another soldier got out of the truck to make them stop their firing. He and a second man walked over to the entrance and tied grey packages around the supports that held the sign. They ran back to the truck and drove a little ways up the road. There was a loud explosion, and the arch supporting the sign collapsed in a cloud of dust. I was frightened by the noise, but mostly for fear they would hurt the weeping tree. When the dust cleared, I was happy to see the tree was fine. After that day, whenever I passed the old hotel, I tried to give the tree some kind of encouragement, and I felt that the tree did the same for me.

Initially, the people in My Tho were happy and welcomed the North Vietnamese victory. They thought it would signal the end of the fighting and suffering. We welcomed the end of the fighting and hoped for peace. But it soon became clear it was only a period of temporary happiness.

The local authorities in My Tho demanded that all citizens register to obtain a document called Ho Khau. Without this permit, you could neither live in your home region with your family nor work. Without it, I would be required to return to my home village of Phu Duc. That would be impossible, for I had already tried. I found that informers had told the authorities in my village that I had become close with the American forces as a result of my wound. Thus, if I returned to Phu Duc, I would be taken to one of several re-education camps. These, I heard, were concentration camps for friends and colleagues of the Americans, where captives were educated about Ho Chi Minh and the Communist party, but were made to work without pay and given very little and very poor food. I was determined not to go, so I hid at my cousin's in My Tho, changed my name, and continued sewing for the tailor.

*   *   *

A full year passed since the appearance of the victorious communists in our delta. We listened to the promises and waited for the better life. But it was slow in coming and times actually grew harder. Although life became more difficult, I was able to survive with my sewing and trips to the market to raise extra money. Whatever my endeavor, I had constantly to avoid the police and hide my identity. When life's burden grew heavy, I escaped to the river, walked along its banks, and thought of peaceful things. Sometimes my brothers took me in their sampans, just to pass the time. The river always gave me new strength and a serenity not found in the busy streets of My Tho.

When I visited my village of Phu Duc, it was only briefly to comfort my mother and bring her money and gifts not available in the countryside. My presence there must be short and unannounced, because those who knew of my past seemed anxious to betray me—perhaps they received compensation. I never knew. It was a puzzle to me how some wretched people could hold such a thing against me, a relationship which had been based only upon good and charitable deeds. The people I knew always thought the Americans had been friendly and charitable, even though they were naïve about our life.

Several times at the market I was harassed, and twice robbed of my market goods by people I saw every day and who somehow knew I was unable to retaliate or complain to the police. They knew I was hiding. It was a humiliating existence, but I kept trying. I thought of the good I had seen in life and concluded I needed to remain an honest person.

One day at the market, I noticed a thin young man looking at me from the row of vendors as he sold sweet potatoes and mangoes. He was wiry and angular, but he had warm eyes which looked at me in an understanding way. I pretended not to notice at first, but his eyes, like a persistent mosquito, always returned. Later I noticed he had been severely wounded in the shoulder and that in healing, his one side had become considerably higher than the other. This gave the impression that he was more handicapped than he really was. Once, after being cheated by a woman who took some of my vegetables without paying, the young man came across the crowded aisle to me.

"Excuse me, Lung," he said, startling me by using my real name. "I saw what happened. I think it would be better if you displayed your goods in a more protected area of the market." He looked at me with kindness as he spoke. The spot I usually chose was in the busy main aisle of the market, which everyone passed, and brought me maximum attention. The young man looked at me. "Your appearance here is attracting troublemakers who recognize your handicap and try to take advantage." As he spoke, he glanced at my leg. "Forgive me for intruding, but I have noticed you and have watched you for some time, and I understand."

Times were hard, and many people were forced into doing things against traditions and the rules of good behavior. I had always avoided the less populated spots in the market, since the police had more time to check documents there, whereas in the main thoroughfare they rarely checked because of the pressing crowds.

"Thank you for helping," I said, a little apprehensive of his use of my real name. He left, and I went home early that day. Later on I noticed the young man moved about as I did, away from visible police checks. Like me, he drifted around the markets in crab-like movements, always keeping distance between himself and the authorities.

One day after I arrived at the market, he helped me to stack my cans of cooking oil. Later he offered to help me carry back those I had not sold. "You are very persistent at selling," he said. "You hide your injury well. If ever you need help, just look my way and signal to me. I can still move quickly, despite the way I look." He smiled with a shy look and added, "You may call me Cong." I noticed he did not say his name was Cong, and decided that like me, he had probably changed his name while in hiding.

Soon we saw each other nearly every day at the market. He said his new name was Nguyen Van Cong. He had originally come from a village in the southern area of Ben Tre Province. I avoided telling him of my home village, and told him I was from My Tho. Cong often accompanied me part of the walk back to my cousin's, to a place where I always turned the wrong way and made excuses so he did not learn where I was really staying. I could not trust anyone in fear of discovery.

One day, while walking together after the market closed, he told me that he had served as an ARVN foot soldier and had been wounded. "You have noticed how I look; it's the result of a wound I received during a battle near Vinh Long during Tet. I was in the hospital there and then sent to an ARVN camp to cook for the soldiers, because I was considered handicapped. I grew quite strong by exercising when I was alone. Now I can run faster and longer than most." He smiled his sly look again and added, "It's helpful now to be faster than the police." He, too, was avoiding the police because, with his wound now mostly healed, he was required to enter the army. Once it was discovered he had been a soldier for the South, he would be required to attend special training and then probably be sent to Kampuchea with the Vietnamese Army.

"I've heard that the soldiers who go to Kampuchea never come back," Cong said. He walked with a hobble which was mostly exaggerated. "I'm rather good at being invisible." That confirmed what I had thought: he was a dodger like me. The similar circumstances drew us closer, and I must say, having someone to share the fear and depression of the long months of evading made us good friends. Soon we began to look for one another at the market. We grew attached, however, still only while away from our homes.

One day, there was a massive sweep and search at the market. Cong intercepted me while I was still in the crowded main road before arriving at the market. "Take a different route, and return home without looking distressed."

I followed Cong's advice, but I noticed two policemen were already walking in our direction. I turned around and saw two more working their way through the crowd towards me. Cong had already slipped away and I thought he was probably safe by now. I worked my way to the edge of the road and quickly discarded the two cooking oil cans I was carrying. I then moved with the crowd, trying to be inconspicuous.

Nevertheless, I was soon herded by the police into a group of twelve people. We were then surrounded by a second pair of policemen who began to cull out individuals for a document check. The police wore the khaki uniforms and sun helmets of the army and carried small pistols on webbed belts. One looked older than the others and seemed to be in charge. As I waited, I noticed the people were not only presenting documents but were also submitting to rough searches by the younger policeman. Two young women searched first were put off to one side and told to wait, and not to move away from the policemen's sight. They were young and attractive women. I grew more frightened, for I had heard stories of the cruelty and depravity of some of the police. It would be too difficult and dangerous to try to evade at that point, so I waited my turn, feeling shocked and discouraged.

Suddenly, I heard a commotion in the street. The sound came closer, and I saw a group of young men running, kicking over the fruit stands, chairs, and vendors' tables lining the street. They created a loud and confusing racket. All four policemen turned and began running in the direction of the disturbance. There was shouting and chaos for a few moments as the police dispersed and tried to catch the running youths. I heard a shout: "Run Lung."

I was shocked and turned towards the sound. A thin figure ran and jumped over a narrow ditch by the road, disappearing into the maze of shelters and stands. The figure ran with one shoulder higher than the other and looked somewhat like a hunchback. He ran swiftly and with the agility and spring of a cat. I instinctively backed away from the group of detainees, still standing in a knot, frozen by the confusion and running. The police were chasing the individuals as I slipped around the side of a shed, down an adjacent path, up another narrow road, and back out onto a road crowded with bicycles. I tried to cross and was nearly run down by a cyclist, who shook his fist at me. I quickly crossed the road and entered another side street, making my way toward the river.

Ever since my escape from the school and the ugly and terrifying scene of battle during the dreadful days of Tet in 1968, I sought the river when in fear. Without exception, it always shielded me from danger, no matter in what form.

I continued walking as fast as I could until I reached the park at the foot of the main boulevard. There were many people lounging and strolling with young children. I tried to melt into the crowd, but imagined all eyes were on me: everyone looking and pointing. "There goes a criminal, evading the police, see her squirm, see her snake her way around, trying to look small, see her hiding, cheating, lying, betraying. Scoundrel, thief, witch. . . ." I tried to get away from what I perceived as the stares and accusing looks of the crowd.

Suddenly, someone grabbed my upper arm and tried to steer me to one side. At first I nearly screamed, then I tried to strike out at the invisible force. It was the sudden change in application of pressure, from the initial feeling to one which actually guided me and supported me, that convinced me the grip was friendly. I stumbled in the direction of the force, gave in to the pressure, and let myself be pushed, then pulled, out of the main park into a line of thick shrubbery. The force on my arm began to lift me, slightly at first, then higher, and taking me by the waist thrust me up, over a small embankment, down a depression on the other side, and into a small covered space beneath a tree sheltering a hut covered with bushes. I felt as if I was flying, then opened my eyes and saw I was being set down on the ground by two strong arms. I saw the dark eyes of Cong as he gently put me down on a soft straw mat. I was exhausted, my breathing was only short gasps. My throat was parched, and I had a terrible throbbing pain in my left leg where my stump rubbed against the mesh of my artificial leg. I wanted to cry, but I was as relieved as I was tired.

Gradually catching my breath, I realized I was in a small hut, hidden from view. It was actually a small house, with some rudimentary furnishings: a table, one stool, a lantern, a kerosene stove, and a small chest. My breathing was normal again and I sat up. Cong, looking embarrassed, smiled and said nothing. His eyes shone with content.

"Searches like this happen more and more now. You must learn to see the warnings and not to get caught. There are always signs, always clues. I never miss them." Cong seemed sure of himself, accurate, yet not cocky. He had mastered the situation yet appeared humble, almost apologetic. I sat in the quiet of the small hut. Cong made tea. He moved with deliberate, fluid motion, with no visible break in the flow when he changed activity from tea making to putting the small room in order. I noticed that when I moved to one side I could look between the crack where the hut and the wide tree met. I could actually see the river and the promenade a short distance away, still crowded with people walking.

"Not a bad vantage point," Cong said softly. "I find it useful to be able to see all around me, yet to be invisible to others. That way I'm never surprised." Cong moved from the small charcoal burner and sat down on the ground next to me. "I'm not the only one living in this fashion. There are many." He smiled again. "It's impossible to see this shelter from any direction. It's well-masked by the larger houses and trees. I know the three adjacent neighbors. We share secrets. I have never been surprised here, never discovered." He smiled in a triumphant way, and I noticed he had a scar on his mouth, making his smile crooked as if he were sharing a secret. The air smelled faintly of charcoal, but it was fresh, and slightly tinged with the smells of the river.

"What do you do when it rains?" I asked. "Surely this spot must flood during the monsoon."

He smiled. "In the monsoon season, I just raise all the furniture by propping large boards underneath. See, I use those six logs as legs." Cong pointed to a pile of smooth round logs stacked neatly in the corner. "In the dry season I use the logs as additional furniture. During the monsoons I become a sort of river dweller and live on stilts," he said.

We sat together for a long time until well after dark. We said little of importance, and waited for the close of the market day. Cong guided me back out to the main boulevard until I got my bearings and said good-night.

"Thank you for saving us back near the market. I don't know what would have happened if you and your friends hadn't distracted the police."

"I'm used to it," he answered. "I once fought these people, now I evade them. They are not so wise, and neither are they so terribly bad. I just don't want to go to Kampuchea." He glided away into the night.

There were many things for me to contemplate, and I lay awake for many hours thinking about all that had transpired. I began to meet Cong often. After a full day in the market, we would slip separately into his little house, and spend long hours talking. He became my first true friend.

Cong liked to talk about the war, and the past. His father and one brother had died in the fighting. His father died a Vietminh in the north, battling the French. His brother fell in the delta near My Tho with the South Vietnamese Rangers. Cong was not a fanatic nor a coward. He believed that the war had been unavoidable and that in time, Vietnam would revert to its earlier status as a great rice producer. He had a strong belief in the Vietnamese peasant farmer. He loved to tell of the ancient Dinh Bo Linh, who as a simple peasant in the tenth century had delivered Vietnam out of a period of chaos caused by competing warlords. Linh had founded a dynasty called Dai Co Viet, "The Kingdom of the Watchful Hawk." Combining clever economic methods with clandestine peasant power groups which paid the occupying Chinese a floating system of tributes of produce and gold. Dinh Bo Linh had used the superior cunning and resourcefulness of the peasant to keep a long period of peace with the militarily superior Chinese. Cong thought a similar tactic was needed now to survive the harsh period of oppression by the communists. Eventually the traditional Vietnamese values would endure and force a return to a government subordinated to free economic forces. He was neither bitter nor angry. He was patient.

Cong equated the long battle for independence against the French, and then between the north and the American-supported south, with the long ideological conflict between the two major religions of Confucianism and Buddhism. That conflict had divided

Vietnam for centuries. "The peasants of Vietnam," said Cong, "need not be concerned with the ideological struggle between capitalism, communism, or a colonial existence. They need only to concentrate on finding the best system for solving their basic needs for land, successful agriculture, irrigation, and security for their villages." He said with a serious look. "If we keep fighting for those goals, the matters of ideology, political systems with sophisticated names and economic plans will automatically fall into place." Cong stood up and paced when he got serious. He spoke like an orator. "I'm in favor of a united Vietnam, regardless of the banner under which it is achieved. I have faith in the Vietnamese farmers, who I believe will eventually force a political system into existence which will be best for the people.

Cong felt the most serious aspect of recent Vietnamese history was not deliverance from the French, nor the war with or against the Americans, nor even the victory of the communist North Vietnamese, but rather the major exodus of educated, trained, and gifted Vietnamese in the tragic migration of the boat people. "That exodus is the most serious phenomenon of modern Vietnamese history," Cong continued. "That massive exodus, damning as it was to the communist victory and supportive as it appears to be to the ideals of American and French democracy and freedom, is the largest issue. Both the French and American sides quit because their populations at home lost the stomach, heart, and will to continue a costly effort." Cong was pacing again. "The serious and irreversable consequences of the migration and mass exodus of tens of thousands of Vietnamese will have a serious impact on the future of Vietnam, regardless of which political system eventually governs the country. The system on top of the heap can always be changed, while the drain of Vietnam's most precious asset, that of its intelligent youth, can be replenished only slowly." Cong grew intense, almost vicious as he repeated, "The crime of the communists was to perpetrate actions which drove their population away by the thousands, risking death and drowning in dilapidated boats in search of a better life. The conditions which caused this exodus must be quickly changed," Cong muttered through clenched teeth. "That is worth killing for." I was frightened of Cong when he was so intense.

One day Cong told me a large sweep and search was planned. The objective was to drive the growing number of young people who were evading the forced conscription out of hiding. Because of the Vietnamese experience in Kampuchea and the growing tension in the north against China, the traditional enemy, efforts to recruit young men for the fighting forces intensified. Cong suggested I remain hidden from the market during this period. He planned to leave My Tho himself and to disappear into the backwaters and canals of the Ben Tre Province he knew so well.

I took Cong's advice. I accumulated enough sewing work to keep myself occupied for some time and stayed off the streets near my cousin's home. Weeks passed, and the entire town lay in a stillness and tension not felt since the days of the fighting. I heard nothing from Cong. Finally, after a month of strict controls, searches, and enforced curfew, the tension eased. I returned to the market, and still found no trace of Cong. I was always circumspect and avoided his hideaway, but as time wore on I could not stand the emptiness caused by his absence and one day I went to his home. I approached as I had done so often in the past. With no one in sight, I crept into his hut.

I was shocked by what I found. All Cong's belongings were strewn on the dirt floor, his chest overturned, all the drawers emptied. I looked about in panic, and just before turning away I spotted a small scarf I had embroidered for him lying among a pile of his possessions in the corner. I scooped it up and ran as fast as I could. I never saw Cong again.

I discovered shortly thereafter that I was with child. It took a long time for me to come to grips with this situation. I had no one to turn to, no one now with whom to share my predicament. I returned to my mother in the village, and although disappointed in me, she arranged for me to stay with her sister in another village near Phu Duc.

The months passed, and despite brief moments of doubt and despair, I was determined to have my child. When I grew doubtful and weak in spirit, I read again a story Cong had shown me of the courage and will of the Trung sisters of the thirteenth-century. One of their followers, a woman named Phung Thi Chinh, had been a dedicated follower and freedom fighter. She had led the Vietnamese forces of the Trung sisters into battle against the Chinese even while she was pregnant. She delivered her baby on the battlefield surrounded by the Chinese. She strapped the newborn baby on her back, took a sword, and led an escape through the encircling Chinese army.

I was determined and clung to my hope and belief in everything good. Perhaps fate would change my life, and I certainly would take no measures to change or end my condition. I gave birth to a beautiful baby girl. After the pain and anguish there came great joy. When I first looked at her, I was greatly moved and relieved. I was determined to nurture her, and to try to give her a better life than mine. I named her Nguyen Diem Trang. I knew someday she would live a peaceful life. I willed it strongly because of my own experience.

*　　*　　*

Time passed and conditions were hard. Although there seemed no end to the suffering, I gained strength from my little daughter. One night I had a dream. In the dream I saw the American Trung Shi Davis, with the kind face and yellow hair. He was wounded and held prisoner by the communists. I also saw Dai Ui Peter, who was trying to help the wounded sailor, but was too far away. I prayed for them when I awoke. Then I had the same dream the following night. The very next day I met Mr. Ha and my life began to change dramatically.

Mr. Ha was an older man who also suffered from a war-induced handicap and was also hiding from the camps. He had worked for the American Army as a translator and had been in hiding since April of 1975. I first met Mr. Ha quite by accident. In My Tho, living under my assumed name of Nguyen Thi Ngan, I was constantly evading the communist police who periodically checked for the Ho Khau permit. They also checked shops and homes for tax records, since the taxes demanded of all citizens were very high.

I had heard some of the lectures and seen some of the indoctrination films shown to residents by the new regime explaining the system of communism. They promised everyone would live under better conditions and everyone would have the same high level of education and benefits. I could not understand when this would come to pass because we lived much the same as before. Everyone went about their own business; the only difference was that the people were taxed more heavily. For individual work, more than half of your earnings were taken. People disappeared frequently, and there was less and less food available in the markets and the shops. The taxation of rice, fruit, vegetables, and pigs from the farmers was so high that there was little left to sell at the market. As a result, people began to cheat and hide food. I myself began cheating in order to survive. I had lied by changing my name—something that was distasteful and against my mother's teachings. Yet this new system caused people to do things they never would have done before, like steal because they were hungry.

One day I was bringing a pile of sewing from the small home where I did the work down the long road to the tailor's shop. On the way, I saw the police had set a checkpoint in the road and were stopping people to check their tax documents for the materials they carried to or from the market. I panicked and turned to leave the main road. As I looked for a familiar side lane, I noticed that a young policeman in uniform had seen me turn abruptly. He rose from the semicircle where the other policemen sat at a small table with a file box. I was still young and quite pretty at the time, and it was not unusual for soldiers and policemen to harass me and to try to get me to come with them. Pursuit usually ended when they saw I had only one leg, but the attention always frightened me. I had heard terrible stories of how the policemen and soldiers did anything they wanted and no one had any way to protest or seek help from the police or authorities. I walked as fast as I could, turned again behind a large building, and stopped to get my breath. I saw the young policeman walk by quickly, then pause and turn in my direction. Again I panicked, dropped my bundle, and tried to run. It was too late. I froze and watched him come toward me. When he reached me, he suddenly looked around to see if anyone was watching. We were alone on the small path, I was petrified. He came forward and stopped in front of me. "Why are you running away?" I didn't answer.

"Where do you live?" he asked sternly. I was still fumbling for an answer when he reached out his hand and felt my hair. He had a wicked look on his face. He grabbed my arm and pulled me to him. "Come with me. What's your name?"

In my fright I accidentally told him my real name. "Nguyen Thi Lung."

"Come with me and we'll talk."

"I can't, I have to go home. My mother's sick," I lied. He pulled me roughly, and I stumbled and fell against a wall. He saw my leg, reached out and felt it with his hand.

"What happened to you?" I didn't answer. He looked around again, then pushed me toward the step to a small hut and began to tear off my trousers.

"Let me see," he said roughly, and he began to feel my leg, then all around both legs and my thighs. I was terrified and pushed him with all my strength. I must have caught him off balance, because he fell back and struck his head on a wire cable holding up a high pole. His sun helmet fell from his head, and as he stooped to pick it up I flung a handful of dirt in his face and began to run.

"You little she-tiger," he shouted, and ran after me. I reached the corner again, hoping to get into the crowded street so there would be other people, but instead I saw the road was nearly empty. It was after the noon hour, and most people were sleeping. I tried another way and just as the young policeman was about to catch me, I collided with a thin man. He was dressed in the typical black cloth trousers and jacket and carried a can of something, either oil or nuc mam. One leg of his black trousers was empty. He carried one wooden crutch which he held level toward the policeman like a gun. His face looked hard. He looked at the policeman then down at my leg, and then said, "Come dear daughter, your mother and I have been waiting for you. We're due at the doctor's shortly."

The policeman stopped abruptly and looked at the man with the outstretched crutch.

"What are you doing? Don't you dare touch this young woman. She is a hero of the people. Don't you see her artificial leg? You buffoon! She's one of the heroes of the My Tho uprising. I should report you to your superiors. Where is your commander?"

The policeman just stared open-mouthed at the man. I looked at the man's eyes. They were black and small, and transformed from kindness, the first look I had seen, to a fierce glare which seemed to frighten the policeman.

"Well, where is your commander?" The young policeman said nothing, backed away, turned quickly, and ran off. "Come quickly," the man said, and he helped me back to where I had dropped my bundle. He led me down a maze of small paths between the area which was close to the central river market, and crowded with small houses. He pulled me inside a small house. There was a smell of incense in the air, and I noticed a small shrine with a statue of the Holy Virgin and a votive light burning before it. These were rare in those days and usually hidden away for special occasions like birthdays.

"Sit down," he said. "I'll get tea." He disappeared into the back behind a hanging curtain. I was still shaking from the encounter and unable to control my hands. I worried about my baby Trang at my cousin's house waiting for my return. The man came back after a few moments carrying a teapot and two glasses. He sat down and quietly poured out the tea. "Are you all right?"

"Yes," I answered, unable to say more.

"The police can be cruel sometimes. Where's your home?" He spoke in a soothing voice and looked as if he was sharing a pleasant thought. Without hesitation, and a sense of trust that did not come often in those times, I told him my story. He listened in silence and drank his tea. He then lit a cigarette, leaned forward slowly, and blew the smoke in the air away from my direction. He nodded as I told him of my wound, the experience in the Catholic school, and the way the Americans had helped me. I even told him about Davis and Dai Ui. He nodded quietly and let me speak. Occasionally he asked short questions, then sat in silence as I finished my story.

Finally, he looked at me with his strong but gentle black eyes glistening with interest and power. No wonder the young policeman had retreated from this man, I thought. He seemed to be equipped with special powers. I thought he might be like the Catholic priests I had known at the school and in Saigon. They had always given me strength by their quiet but strong presence.

"You've had good fortune," he said, smiling. He rose to his feet, went to the corner and rummaged through some papers, then returned with a single sheet and held it out for me to read. It was a certificate of appreciation for twelve years service with the American Army as a translator and interpreter. The worn paper had a large seal, some signatures in English, and at the top, a large American flag entwined with the old South Vietnamese flag of red and yellow. The symbol reminded me of the painted sign which had hung above the Victory Hotel entrance. There were other symbols I did not understand. He took the paper back, handling it very carefully, covered it again with white tissue paper, and returned it to his corner.

"Did you have to go to a re-education center?" I asked.

He looked at me and smiled, again with his secret smile, and laughed, "No, I was supposed to, but I evaded, and am still avoiding them. They are not very clever, too bureaucratic. You see, I have a way of proving I'm not really here." He smiled again. "They can't seem to find where I am really, so they leave me alone." I could not quite follow his words, but it did not matter. I was relieved to share my story with someone else who had a connection to hide. I felt I could trust him, and he seemed to trust me.

"My name is Than Van Ha," he said, as if settling down to share everything.

"Do you have a family?" I asked.

"No, they're all gone now: two sons, lost in the ARVN, one daughter and wife lost during the My Tho Tet fighting in 1968. But that was long ago. I live quite comfortably alone."

"Could we meet again sometime?" I asked. "I'm in a hurry, my daughter is waiting for me." Mr. Ha nodded in agreement.

"Come here anytime, but stay on the main street and try to travel during the busy hours of the day. The police are unreliable and dangerous. Come again and we can talk."

I gathered my sewing, said good-bye to Mr. Ha, and walked back to my cousin's house. My cousin was only fifteen minutes away from Mr. Ha. That night I had the third dream about Mr. Davis, the same exact dream I had the nights before. I decided to tell the dream to Mr. Ha the next time we met. That night I slept well, a deep and warmly delicious sleep. I had a new friend, one who was in a similar situation.

I went back to Mr. Ha's house a few days later. We talked for a long time. I told him more of my experiences with the Americans, my drive to Saigon, the stay with the kind Co Yen in the rehabilitation center, and the first night of the Tet Offensive. He listened as usual, in silence. He then told me stories of his time spent as an interpreter. We continued to meet several times each week, exchanging stories and unknowingly, giving each other new strength. I told Mr. Ha about my three dreams. When I finished, Ha was quiet for awhile and then looked at me.

"You're a very lucky young woman. Your good fortune is not over yet. You must be vigilant and take every chance you get. Don't let opportunity pass. You will certainly succeed some day," he said. I thought of his words often. They kept me enthusiastic and hopeful. At least I was free and not in a camp, I thought.

Once during a meeting he told me about the boat people. These were people who left everything behind and escaped Vietnam by boat to find a better way of life. Ha said that any citizen who could obtain three to four bars of twenty-four karat gold could buy a place on a boat.

"The boats depart from ports on the seacoast, like Vung Tau, Cam Ranh, and Nha Trang. They can also be found in other lesser ports," Ha said, "But theft, betrayal, and piracy plague the would-be escapees, and many are never heard from again."

"Do you know anyone who got away on the boats?" I asked.

"Yes, many," he answered, and he began to tell me stories of the escapes. I sat listening breathlessly as he told me one after another.

One story in particular was of a colleague from his days as an interpreter who, after several attempts to escape during the evacuation in March and April of 1975, had returned to My Tho and began a detailed plan with friends to build a boat on the river near town. They worked for one whole year building, gathering supplies, and choosing a crew. Finally one night they slipped away, sailed down river, and into the sea. Two years later, Ha received a letter from his friend who had reached America. He subsequently received several other letters, which described in detail the voyage and their adventures. The story seemed to be endless. There were accounts of meeting pirates from Thailand on the South China Sea, of torture, rape, and of the slow deaths of some of the crew members. Day after day, I returned to hear more of the story. Ha's friend, nearly dead, had managed to turn the tables on the pirates along with one remaining member of his crew. He killed them and took their boat, reaching the shores of Malaysia after nearly two months at sea. He then told of his long ordeal there in a refugee camp, from where he escaped to hide out near Java. From there he carried out a long correspondence with Vietnamese relatives in America and was finally accepted in the American Embassy in Jakarta and given a refugee visa. The key to his acceptance was his preserved certificate of service with the Americans, like Ha's, which he had kept intact throughout the voyage. He now owned a restaurant in Chicago.

*   *   *

One day when I came to visit, Mr. Ha was fixing tea as always. He was very excited. He told me about a new program agreed upon between the Vietnamese authorities and the American government. It was designed to ease the terrible loss of life caused by the large number of Vietnamese leaving the country by boat. I recalled the many stories I had heard from others, including my cousin, about those who had paid for passage out of Vietnam by boat with their four gold sticks. Mr. Ha's eyes glowed more brightly than ever before.

"Lung," he said, looking intensely at me. "You have to get your story down on paper. I can translate your words to English. My English is still good. You see I still read the books I received as gifts from the American soldiers."

"Then what?" I asked.

"Well, let's take one step at a time and trust in the future. You must begin to write, and recall as much as you can. If you want, you can do it here with me. That way I can start translating immediately."

I was afraid to become too excited about Mr. Ha's ideas, but he was the only ray of hope I had. I went to him every other day and we would sit, sometimes at night, and go over the account.

"Do you have any papers, any letters, any evidence to lend support to your story?" Ha asked.

"None," I answered. "I have nothing to show."

"Well, we'll come up with something. Keep looking," he said. We continued to meet.

One day, while preparing some sewing to go to the tailor, I was looking for more buttons. I reached up to my cupboard, and looked through an old box where I kept the few treasures I still had. There I found an old folded piece of newspaper. I took it and carefully opened it. It was the newspaper photograph of me taken in My Tho by the American journalist several days after I had returned from the rehabilitation center in Saigon with my new leg. It showed me with both Dai Ui and Trung Shi Davis sitting in the jeep in which we had traveled to Saigon. I used to look at the picture often years ago, but I had hidden it in the box, since I could not safely show it to anyone else. It might even be cause to throw me into the re-education camps. I shuddered, then put the picture, still folded, into the hem of my loose fitting shirt. I took it with me the next time I went to Mr. Ha.

"That's it!," he exclaimed when he saw the picture. "That might do it. We must make a copy of it. I can do that. I have a friend in a photo shop. Will you trust me to keep it for a week?" he asked. "I'll have it back to you then and we can use a copy, smaller of course, for the story." I waited and trusted.

Finally the letter was finished, the picture copied, and all was ready. I asked Mr. Ha why he did not do one for himself. He replied with his far-off look that he was too old, and did not want to leave.

"I belong here," he said. "Some day this may all end. Then I'll be needed. I often get the feeling that things will change, and I'll become vital for the country. No, I don't want to go anywhere. But you are young, and you can go far."

I never quite understood how Mr. Ha kept up his undying enthusiasm, but he did. He often spoke to me about the things the Americans had taught him and about the things he had read in the books they had given him. He said once that the strong leaders of North Vietnam, who had succeeded in uniting the country despite the cost in human suffering, would probably change their tactics when they had a chance to deliberate after the fighting stopped. He felt that a greater good would come to Vietnam because of leaders who were enlightened people and capable of change. They were, he believed, much more enlightened, educated, and wiser than the leaders of the South, who for some reason never quite grasped the true issues of the war, and who had never truly represented the spirit of the people who had suffered so long at the hands of the French colonials and then the Japanese.

"How were the Americans different from the French?" I asked.

"Ah, that's a marvelous question, Lung, one I could go on and on about." He drew closer and began a beautiful lecture on the differences between the involvement of the Americans compared with the long colonial period under the French. "But the best example of the difference between the cultural effect is this," he said beaming. It was visibly his favorite subject.

"The French gave to the Vietnamese the assets the French called 'the resources of modern civilization,' which included modern legal codes and a cash economy, where the ownership of money, land, and goods was of primary importance. This was done while the wealthy Vietnamese landowners retained the power and exploited their countrymen as peasants. All this happened while the French themselves lived on a level highly elevated and removed. The French were fierce taskmasters, but also careful to retain control of key assets to preclude the Vietnamese from becoming self-sufficient. A good example of this was evident in the power-generating stations of all the major cities under the French. French engineers held the key positions, which dealt with the highly technical subject of the generating plants. While the Vietnamese were employed in the plants and ran them, no Vietnamese ever became a manager. Control was retained by French engineers to keep a separation and to perpetuate the segregation. The first thing the American engineers did was teach the local Vietnamese how to run the plants at all levels and after a short time, the plants were run entirely by Vietnamese."

According to Ha, this was the best example of the difference and the primary reason the American experience in the twenty years between 1955 and 1975 probably left a larger technological imprint on the Vietnamese than the decades of the French colonial period. "The French gave us an appreciation of culture and learning, but that was limited to a small percent of the upper class Vietnamese landowners and merchants who were sustained in their positions by the French. The Americans, on the other hand, with their unlimited enthusiasm and naïveté, and limited in most cases to single-year asignments, left the Vietnamese with greater roles in the fields of agriculture, engineering, economics, and civic government. The white-collar bureaucracy that permeated the French system was absent under the Americans."

Ha seemed to be greatly uplifted by his oration. He stood and raised his arms. "The effect of the short period of exposure to the Americans has already begun to exert itself on the Vietnam of today. We hold the American system of free economy and entrepreneurship as a role model."

"Lung," he said, "Vietnam will one day take its place among the leading economies of the Pacific, once the leaders who succeeded in winning this war refocus their dream on the goals of a free market. When that happens, the shift to a democracy will follow, I'm as certain as I am standing here."

Ha sat down, exhausted by his talk. He was at his best, I thought, when he got all wound up in his philosophy. His face was gleaming and his eyes were bright. Ha felt the communists would soon see that the traditions of the Vietnamese people could lead them back to the market at which they had been so good in the past. If that transition were made, the quality of life would again improve.

At the time I never believed Mr. Ha's conviction about the future. I had seen too much blood and suffering at the hands of first the Vietcong, and now the communist police. How could that lead to anything good?

But Mr. Ha continued to talk to me about the Vietnam of tomorrow. He had a solid enthusiasm which was so alive and on fire that it was difficult to argue with him. We had sessions like this often and, as the time passed, I grew to enjoy his vision, and even to believe.

*   *   *

The time finally came when our letter was ready. Mr. Ha had carefully made three copies of the letter and the photo enclosure. He addressed one to the American Embassy in Bangkok, Thailand. Another he addressed to United Press International in Hong Kong, an address he took from an old business card given to him by some newsmen during his days as an interpreter. He recalled how he had accompanied the Americans while they took the newsmen around. The American army had treated the journalists as very special people. Ha had not understood at the time why the Americans, even the colonel, seemed to fear the journalists. In any case, the impression was not lost on him, and he assumed it was another of the many strange attitudes of the Americans which he did not understand. He had kept the card of one of the press members and used the same name and address, even though it was then 1980, a good ten years since he had first received it. But Mr. Ha did not know to whom to address the third letter, but he kept it just in case.

Mr. Ha disappeared for several days. When I saw him again, he was beaming. "Your letters have gone. Now we must just wait patiently. In the meantime, I will think of what to do with the third letter."

Weeks passed and then months. I visited Mr. Ha often. Once I had a terrible fright. I had not visited Mr. Ha for a few days, and when I approached his house I saw several people standing around the door. I slowly walked closer but stayed in the side shadow. I heard people muttering how terrible it was and what a scandal. I could wait no longer and rushed to the doorway. I peered inside and saw the place was a mess. It had been ransacked and demolished. Everything inside was strewn around or smashed. There were bed clothes on the ground and papers and broken dishes lying everywhere. I stood inside the door for a long time before noticing Mr. Ha in the corner lying on the ground. The other people had gone and I was alone with the poor man. His face was bleeding but he seemed otherwise unhurt. I helped him up, found his crutch, and helped him straighten his clothes. I was afraid to ask what happened. He looked up at me and smiled his secret smile. He knelt down and from under his bed, pulled a straw mat. From a seam in the side, he pulled his old certificate and our third letter. He looked pleased with himself, and said quietly, "They were so clumsy, they didn't search cleverly enough."

I never knew exactly what happened that day, but I knew Mr. Ha had enemies who meant him harm. I continued to visit him nonetheless.

Chapter VII

The Return

Peter

After the simple change of command ceremony in Canh Tho, I left the PBR section and returned to Saigon via helicopter. There I processed out for return to the States. I felt a sense of uneasy calm. For some reason, I did not feel I should be going home with all the unfinished business at hand. There was, after all, a war going on. I was both elated and sad at the same time. Elated to be alive and sad to be leaving the river section troops. I was proud of their record, yet relieved that I would not oversee the loss of any more men. Remaining for a second year on the rivers was not professionally viable for me, since I was expected to return to the active seagoing navy.

I was shocked back to reality as I waited in the transient hall in Tan Son Nhut for a flight back to Travis Air Force Base in California. Mortar rounds began to land on the sprawling air base and I dove for cover, thinking how ironic it would be to be killed or maimed within hours of lifting off for home. I remembered hearing of this before. I huddled under the useless protection of a cot in the waiting room when I heard an Air Force sergeant call off a list of names, including mine.

"Grab your gear and haul it to the far side of the flight line. If you leave something, you can't come back." As I ran with my seabag, I thought of his words. What was I leaving that I could not return for? The unfinished struggle, the villages and outposts on the rivers and canals still holding out for survival? The Vietnamese who had trusted us, hoped and still held out against all the odds? I left more there than I realized. I ran across the spacious flight line, ignoring the explosions and falling debris.

I was one of only six passengers in a huge, green C-141 with a cargo bay lined with bright aluminum military coffins. Numb with fatigue and the heat, I had the recurring fear of being struck by flying shrapnel, becoming a useless casualty of the war, hit while enroute home. I strapped myself into one of the two rows of three-abreast seats and spent the next twelve hours staring at the coffins in the overhead. As we flew over the Pacific, my mind whirred through the past months. I relived the ambushes, saw the wounded, the faces of endless lines of Vietnamese, the sailors, the PRUs, and the SEALs. I heard the whine of the PBR engines, the sound of the 50-caliber machine guns popping, and the murmur of the people on crowded water craft. I smelled the betel nut of the women, the nuc mam, and the stench of the wounded and dead. I saw the beautiful Co Yen in Saigon and the eyes of Lung, which never showed pain. I wondered where she was as I slipped into a light sleep. In my dreams I saw the bodies moving inside the silver coffins lying before me in the giant cargo bay.

*   *   *

The aircraft touched down at Travis on April 7, 1968. I walked from the aircraft, dragging my seabag, and looked out over the San Francisco Bay area. It did not feel like home. I caught a bus waiting to take returnees to the commercial airport in San Francisco, where I was booked on a flight for San Diego for the beginning of my debriefings.

When I arrived at the airport and climbed off the bus with a handful of other returning troops, I noticed a demonstration underway on the road outside the airport. Some protestors were gathered, several hundred by the looks of it, to meet a delegation of some unknown politicians arriving on a U. S. Government aircraft with the flag and "United States of America" emblazoned on the tail. To this day I do not know who had arrived, but the crowd was unruly, unwashed and, to me, totally alien. I stared in amazement as I read some of the signs: "Stop the War," "Hey, Hey, LBJ, How Many Kids Did You Kill Today?" I stood and watched the crowd with no feeling. The knot of young people for some reason swayed and spilled over in our direction. Suddenly, I was engulfed by the crowd's pushing and screaming. The young people swept by, some chanting, some screaming slogans I could not make out. Some were silent, smoking and drinking beer from cans. I was lost in a swirling sea of American youth of the late sixties, from which I felt totally removed.

The atmosphere was more of a carnival than a protest. Each participant carried or chanted his own slogan. There was no sign of leadership or organization, only a deep-rooted anger and frustration. Suddenly, I was approached by a girl with a bandanna-wrapped head, long stringy hair, and clothes looking like they had never been changed. She thrust her face in mine and screamed, "Hey soldier boy, what're the ribbons for?" Then she reached out and tore off a row of ribbons from my summer white uniform. Another, a boy with a bare chest and long hair, tore off my hat and threw it on the ground.

I had not noticed that the other troops from the bus had quickly disappeared, and I stood alone except for a young black soldier still in his jungle fatigues. Someone had pushed him down onto the pavement. Instinctively I grabbed for him, looking for some solidarity. A chant started, and I realized the two of us, too dazed to move from the scene as the other soldiers had done, had become the center of a small side demonstration. "Baby killers, baby killers. . ." they chanted. The faces were contorted and reflected genuine hate and a fervor I had never seen before. I was frightened. As if in a bad dream, I tried to blink the scene from my mind and to run away, but the press of chanting bodies prevented escape. My fear turned to panic, then anger. I remember backing up to the other remaining soldier, who had struggled to his feet, fists clenched, and trembling visibly. His hat was gone and the front of his uniform was torn. He looked as frightened as I did. We stood leaning against one another, until something inside me snapped and I lashed out with my fists. My ally, an unknown soldier from some unnamed unit, was cast with me into close partnership. We both swung wildly. I remember connecting only once, with all my strength on the chin of a bearded visage. Blood sprayed my hands and face. The melee continued for some time. I felt kicks, scratches, and blows, but none seriously damaging. The next thing I knew, I was being held by two blue-clad policemen. The soldier next to me had at least three policemen trying to restrain him. The crowd had dispersed and several civilian youths were also being restrained. One sat on the ground, blood streaming from his nose, while a second lay on his side holding his groin. The police pushed us into a room inside the airport where we were held in "protective custody" until our flights left. The next weeks brought a series of events for which I was poorly prepared.

*   *   *

Several days after returning to San Diego, I was sent back to Mare Island for a debriefing at the PBR training center. The training pipeline for providing replacements for the river patrol force was similar to what I had gone through more than a year before. Now the boats in use were the Mark II PBRs, a much improved and faster boat, which could mount a heavier 20-millimeter gun in place of the forward 50-caliber machine gun mounts. These guns packed significantly more punch and were more versatile against bunkered positions on the canals and rivers.

I spent a full day answering questions from the staff, and then spoke to a large group of trainees in the last weeks of their training. The questions asked by the young officers were primarily technical in relation to the performance of the boats, the living conditions, the weaknesses and the vulnerabilities of the operations, and the state of morale. I answered most questions in good humor and in good taste. One young engineer stood up and asked, "Sir, what would you have done differently if you had it to do all over again?"

I thought, and unable to find a clever answer, looked at him, "I would have stayed there until it was over."

*   *   *

After the debriefings, I was released and able to wander around San Diego for the evening. Instinctively, I returned to the PBR sailors' old haunt, Gilbert's Tavern, and watched the evening crowd. I felt good for the first time since I had returned. After a seafood dinner, I observed young Americans enjoying their evening. I sat in silence as the bartender turned on the late TV news. I watched as the announcer analyzed the California Democratic primary election returns. It appeared Robert Kennedy had won. Suddenly the newsman announced there had been a shooting in a hotel kitchen and Senator Kennedy had been shot and was in serious condition. I remained in my seat for a moment in shock, and then walked out into the street. I looked around and kept walking, unable to focus on anything in particular. My thoughts turned to the now seemingly insignificant people I had spent the last year with—the Vietnamese. While participating in their struggle, I had considered them important. Now that I was removed from that ordeal, separated by thousands of ocean miles, their importance had left me. They were now far away and secondary to our dilemma at home. I remembered Lung, and how she looked the day we said good-bye. She was always positive, displaying a tenacious moral courage which to me seemed naïve, perhaps even futile, given her situation following the loss of her leg. How would Americans fare in such a situation, I wondered? Her country was hopelessly embroiled in a chaotic war. Her only allies came and fought on her side for one year at a time, then packed their bags and disappeared back to their comfortable land of plenty and peace.

I wondered what had happened to Lung. Had she really perished during Tet? Did she die bravely, or had she escaped to safety? A strong ache developed within me when I thought of Lung, and it continued for many years. Was there really comfort and peace in America? I walked on, losing myself in the city lights.

*   *   *

For many years following my return from the rivers of Vietnam, I looked for a clear explanation of what really transpired there. It did not seem possible that an effort mounted by a country with America's military history and with the wonderful talent of our youth could go so remarkably awry. But I refused to accept the widely-held notion that the entire American effort in Vietnam was a defeat from which no good resulted.

When viewed against the backdrop of the eventual implosion and fall of the rest of the communist world, which is still more than a decade behind Vietnam in the transition to a market economy, the Vietnamese experience is even more remarkable. In a few years, Vietnam will take her place as a vibrant and healthy economic force in the new Pacific family of nations. This transition by Vietnam, to a system Americans themselves embrace, did not come about by chance or without the positive influence of the large American effort which spanned the turbulent years from the French defeat in 1954 until the cessation of all U.S. assistance to South Vietnam in 1974. The attitude of the Vietnamese today is ample evidence of the American influence during their years of struggle. The efforts by American experts in the fields of agriculture, economics, commerce, medicine, engineering and, to a large extent, defense and security, played a profound role in the delicate transformation of Vietnam. The lasting effect of this immense transmittal of expertise and values to the people of Vietnam during the war years was demonstrated initially by the mass exodus of the boat people, and the failure of the re-education camps run by the victorious communist Vietnamese. Neither the long-feared domino effect in Asia nor the predicted massive bloodletting occurred following the fall of Saigon. Instead, there was a pause, and then slow movement forward as the Vietnamese recovered from a long history of violence.

The American sailors feel that their efforts on the rivers and canals of the Mekong Delta were not in vain. Those Americans involved over the years in the long endeavor of training, educating, and administering to the Vietnamese made an indelible impact. It is to these participants that Vietnam has eventually paid an instinctive tribute by seeking closer economic and cultural ties with America.

But in 1968 my professional navy involvement with Vietnam had ceased. I was in a new field in the navy and moved from assignment to assignment with a detached attitude toward the festering conflict in Southeast Asia. I avoided thinking about the events of 1967 and 1968. In 1973 I was in Pearl Harbor serving on the Third Fleet staff when our prisoners of war were released. I went to Hickam Air Force Base and watched with the crowds as each large C-141 Starlifter rolled to a stop on the massive air field and disgorged its cargo of newly-released American POWs. These men's lives had been permanently altered by incarceration, which in some cases was as long as six or seven years. These certainly were the real American heroes of the war. I was relieved to see many classmates and friends return after the long periods of imprisonment.

I was still in Hawaii in April of 1975, when Saigon fell to the North Vietnamese. I felt little except curiosity. What had become of all those villages and outposts we had defended along the Mekong? Where were Co Thuong, the interpreter, Dai Ui Chuk from Kien Van, Sergeant Dinh from the river police, and the others? The phenomenon of the mass exodus of the boat people had been underway for some time, and I read the accounts with mixed emotions and with little hope or anticipation. What had happend to Lung? The ache to know about her began to grow into a fantasy.

My last involvement in the navy with Vietnamese events took place while embarked as part of the ship's company aboard the USS *Enterprise* on a deployment to the western Pacific in 1978. The ship was operating in and out of Subic Bay and was headed for a deployment to the Indian Ocean via Malacca. One night, while operating in the Philippine Sea, *Enterprise* surveillance aircraft reported a small craft drifting in the moderate seas with about twenty people aboard. It was a heavily laden motorized junk. *Enterprise* followed the standing Seventh Fleet directive regarding encounters with Vietnamese boat people and approached the sampan to investigate the condition of those on board. The policy at the time was to render assistance only if human life was in danger. As the ship's intelligence officer, I was directed by the captain to be present at the starboard gangway when the *Enterprise* went alongside the junk to evaluate the situation.

A detachment of ship's company Marines, headed by a young lieutenant, waited with me as the wallowing craft was rowed to an illuminated accommodation ladder leading down to the water from a gangway. Luckily the weather was calm making the maneuver only marginally dangerous. To moor at sea alongside an aircraft carrier with sides extending more than eighty feet up to the flight deck and another eighty to the pilot house is no easy feat. When I descended the ladder with the Marines, we could see the condition of the junk was grim. It was out of fuel, overcrowded, and had only a few inches of freeboard showing. If the weather worsened even slightly, the overloaded craft would certainly founder. The Marine party assigned to investigate the craft with me was communicating with the bridge via sound-powered phones.

"The captain wants a report on the condition of the people in the boat," a voice shouted down the ladder. The lieutenant and I, wearing bulging kapok life jackets, reached the bottom of the long accommodation ladder and peered into the boat. The scene was familiar to me. It was like looking deep into the past. Twenty-three Vietnamese huddled together in the boat, eyes wide with fright, looking totally helpless and trusting. The odors of Vietnam hung in the air and sent my mind racing back to the rivers and the hundreds of sampans we had searched from our PBRs. I gaped in silence at the scene.

"Bridge wants to know how many souls aboard," someone shouted down the ladder.

"Twenty-three, including two babies and five children."

"What's their condition?"

"Wet, cold, and scared."

"What's the condition of the boat?"

"Engine's out of service—plus no fuel left."

"Captain wants to know if the people are in any danger." I looked at the Marine lieutenant, too young to have been in Vietnam. This Marine would not know the feeling of entering combat with a life expectancy of sixteen seconds, like other Marine lieutenants. "Sir, we have to unload the boat to look at the condition of the hull to see what's wrong with the engine," he said.

"Okay," I said. "Tell the bridge we're going to unload the people and have a look at the boat to see if we can get the engine going. Tell the bo'suns to send down some gasoline."

The tiny Vietnamese streamed up the long swaying ladder. Several more Marines came down to help carry the children. When the boat was empty, the lieutenant and I took the Vietnamese leader back onto the junk and looked at the engine. The swells sent water cascading into the boat. It looked hopeless. Even if they could get the motor running to make headway, the boat certainly would not make the nearest landfall with twenty-three people aboard. It was cold, and after standing in the wet hull for a few minutes, we were soaked through.

"Sir, bridge wants to know the condition of the junk."

"Shit," I said to the lieutenant. "Send up for a fire axe." We motioned the Vietnamese man to leave the boat, and he lost no time scrambling up the ladder. A long-handled red fire axe came down the ladder, passed hand over hand by the Marines. The lieutenant handed it to me.

"What're you going to do with that, Commander?"

"Turn the other way," I answered. "Sometimes things just need to be done without asking." I swung the axe several times at the transom of the junk and knocked the engine into the water. "Get back on the ladder," I shouted to the Marine, and gave the hull several more whacks with the axe. Sea water began to gush into the wooden hull. Happily, no one on the *Enterprise* bridge could see the junk beneath the overhang of the flight deck and the large sponson. Nor could the ship's executive officer, who had finally joined the group at the top of the accommodation ladder. He stood nervously directing the activity sixty feet above the junk.

"Boat's sinking," I shouted, then jumped onto the ladder's platform. The lieutenant grabbed my arm to steady me. I cut the line holding the junk to the ship. The rapidly sinking hulk drifted away from the side of the grey steel carrier and was soon totally awash.

"Sir, XO wants to know what the hell you're doing with an axe down there," shouted another Marine on the ladder. I looked at the lieutenant, whose eyes brightened with sudden understanding.

"What axe?" I shouted up the ladder, and slid the red fire axe into the water and watched it drop from sight into the dark sea. We climbed up to the sponson and looked down. The junk capsized and then drifted away into the night.

The XO was suddenly standing before me. "What the crap happened, Peter?" he shouted. The exec wasn't a terribly bright officer, but he held the world record in push-ups, so that was all right.

"Well, Sir," I began, "we were trying to fix the engine and she started to sink."

"What were you doing with the goddamn fire axe, Peter?" I looked at the young Marine who looked frightened, wondering whether I was going to lie to the XO.

"Sir, you know I used to be a chief engineer and spent a year on the Mekong River climbing on and off those junks. I know how temperamental Vietnamese gas engines can be. I was just using the axe to fix it, Sir," I finished with a straight face.

"Where's the axe, Peter?" he asked.

"I dropped it while trying to evacuate the boat, Sir."

The XO stared at me a moment, then at the lieutenant. A smile of understanding spread across his face.

"Bridge, this is the XO, junk sank. The refugees are on their way to sick bay for a medical check. Tell the main galley to bring hot soup and tea to sick bay." The exec looked at me and shook his head, then made his way back to the bridge.

The lieutenant looked at me. "Where were you in Vietnam, Sir?"

"Everywhere where things were screwed up," I answered.

"Were you ever wounded?"

"No," I replied, "not where it shows."

Chapter VIII
Deliverance

Saigon, March 1981

Nine-year-old Ba skulked from alley to shop front on the crowded Tu Do Street in the capital once called Saigon—now Ho Chi Minh City. He enjoyed doing work for Mr. Ha. The assignment meant an exciting escape from My Tho, a trip in a crowded bus north along Highway 4, and enough piasters in his pocket to buy the Chinese soup that warmed his stomach and made him feel brave.

When he first spotted the strange gangling foreigners, now rare in the city, he knew the trip would be a success, the rest of the chore easy. Foreigners always seemed too disconnected to notice him sticking notes or envelopes inside their clothing. Each time he had made deliveries in the past—he had done it often—he achieved total surprise, and was never detained by the foreigner or, more importantly, by the dangerous military police. The police seemed to be everywhere in the capital city, patrolling in their khaki sun helmets and army sandals. Ba worried about the police. They were harsh on wrongdoers, even the young. Ba was almost ten and able to attend a state school in addition to the secret lessons with Mr. Ha.

Ba slipped out onto the main road and spotted a man and a woman walking ahead of him, too large to be Vietnamese. They moved slowly, their arms swinging more loosely than the locals'. Ba rushed his steps and wove expertly through the morning crowd. If he could make another perfect delivery, he would be on a bus back to My Tho before dark, and with Mr. Ha before the old man turned in for the night. That meant another bowl of steaming noodle soup in the corner restaurant in My Tho the next morning.

153

Ba scanned the street for police; there were none in sight. He drew closer to the two foreigners and heard their strange language, curiously coarse and louder than Vietnamese voices. Ba's keen eyes took in the size and shape of the foreigners' clothing; easy prey, he observed. The woman wore a baggy skirt, and carried a large leather bag and a camera dangling on a long colorful strap below her chest.

Sylvana Foa, an American journalist working for United Press International out of Hong Kong, had made several trips to Saigon to cover the exodus of the boat people. During the visits, her actions had been carefully followed by government surveillants. Despite the scrutiny, Sylvana noticed she was often followed by young children, somehow deducing she was American. Several times children had thrust messages or letters discreetly into the folds of her clothing. Sylvana observed that most messages were addressed to family members or friends who had fled the country by boat to fates unknown. On this trip in April of 1981, Sylvana and her partner, Neil Davis from NBC, were careful to wear baggy clothes with multiple folds and deep pockets to enhance fielding information about the dramatic escapes. The two Americans were strolling down Tu Do Street in the morning rush before catching a minibus to the airport for their departure flight.

Ba glanced around, then stole quickly into a side street, raced to the left behind several shops, and out again toward the street, arriving slightly ahead of the approaching foreigners. Ba paused, breathing faster after the sprint, and waited until the two strangers strolled past. He selected the woman as the most vulnerable; she had the fullest clothes. When the targets were five steps past, Ba darted out, brushed the lady as he ran by, and thrust the brown envelope into a deep floppy pocket of her skirt. Ba quickly ran away, neatly dodging an oncoming motor scooter, then turned left and darted back into an alley. The mission was completed.

On the way to the airport, Sylvana felt her pocket, realizing the young urchin who had brushed by her earlier on Tu Do Street had passed a letter, probably another forlorn attempt to smuggle words of hope and encouragement out of the country. On the flight back to Hong Kong, Sylvana opened the letter. It was neatly typed and very well written, apparently on an ancient typewriter. A yellowed newspaper article, carefully folded and wrapped in thin rice paper, fell from the envelope. The faded article was from a September, 1967 issue of the New York Daily News and included a photograph of a young Vietnamese girl with an American navy lieutenant wearing a black beret. The caption told of a ten-year-old girl receiving an artificial leg with the help of the sailors from a U.S. Navy river patrol unit based in My Tho. There were no names given.

Lung

The first good news came in an oblique way—not a letter, not a message, but a search of my cousin's house. For some reason, I had again been singled out as a target of interest—I hoped not because of the letters, which Mr. Ha had dispatched somehow earlier in the year. He did not discuss the method of mailing. It was, like his other deeds, not for detailed discussion. But I had heard the young boy, Ba, boast to friends that he had been entrusted by Mr. Ha to act as courier, delivering important documents under shady conditions to foreigners in Saigon.

While I was out with Trang, now a powerful package of love, beauty, and muscle, our house was visited by the uninvited. The first sign was the slanted pole holding the door in the orderly entrance. It had been moved. There was the usual smell of betel nut coming from the direction of the elderly woman who shared the shelter of the grass-covered veranda. The woman had been a source of displeasure for some time. She was always watching us and asking questions. I felt she might be an informer. Cigarette smoke, not normal in our house, hung in the air like a blanket. Our sandals, normally aligned neatly in a single row before the entrance, had been knocked askew. Chicken parts, discarded earlier, lay in a pile on the metal pan in the corner. Two dogs, usually too shy to forage inside the house, were enjoying the scraps, encouraged no doubt by the unusual amount of debris strewn on the dirt floor.

"They came again," the nosey old woman muttered. "It's time you registered and faced paying what you owe, you little eel."

I ignored the woman, stood in the door, and recoiled at the scene of chaos in our little home, normally neat and carefully organized. I straightened out our belongings and prepared tea and a meal of rice and chicken I got from the market on the way home. I was tired from the long afternoon in the market and the walk around My Tho with Trang. She had been full of energy and unresponsive to pacification. The unwelcome visit could have been the work of the young ruffians from down the road, or worse, the authorities. We sat in the quiet of the late evening drinking tea. I thought of tomorrow's work.

Suddenly the young boy, Ba, thrust his head into the hut. His head was dusty and looked like a porcupine, short black hairs jutting out like tar-covered prongs. He whispered, "Please to visit Mr. Ha. Now and not too much later."

First startled and angered, then intrigued by the interruption, I dismissed the boy after rewarding him with a chunk of chicken. My cousin, Phuong, agreed to stay with Trang. I hurried out the door.

Mr. Ha was sitting, reading under a dim lamp. He sat with his back to the corner, facing the door, ready, as he always said, to scare off intruders. He looked up as I entered, never was startled, always looking as if he knew all along of my presence. In his eyes I could see that he had something to tell me. He was unable to hold a secret long when I was there.

"What is it?" I asked.

"I've heard," he smiled, "from the world out there." He motioned with a sweep of his arm. "You have been recognized for your suffering."

"Stop teasing please, Mr. Ha. What do you mean?"

"We've heard from the press. Look," he waved an envelope. The letter read:

> To Nguyen Thi Lung. I received your letter and story. You must send another letter to the enclosed address. I am forwarding a copy of this one, but the program office needs a request directly from you. We have begun a search for the sailors in the picture. If successful, they might become your sponsors.

The letter was signed Sylvana Foa, United Press International, Hong Kong. I looked at Ha, stunned. "Am I dreaming?" I asked, well aware that it was real; how could he have fabricated the address?

Mr. Ha stood up slowly. "You see, it's the signal we've been waiting for. Tomorrow I'll send the third letter to this address: Orderly Departure Program, Mr. Donald Colin, American Embassy, Bangkok, Thailand."

Triumph

Peter

Fourteen years after I left Vietnam, while serving as U.S. Naval Attaché in Belgrade, Yugoslavia, I received a cable from the Seventh Fleet flagship written by the fleet intelligence officer, my Annapolis classmate, Ted Schaeffer, saying that my picture was circulating in newspapers around the Far East with the caption: "Young Vietnamese woman seeks American foster father. Do you know this man?" Ted's message continued, "The picture is either of you or a twin. The last three letters of your name are visible on your uniform shirt. Good luck."

I couldn't believe my eyes. A second message arrived two days later from the U.S. Embassy in Bangkok.

> To: Commander Peter A. Huchthausen, U.S. Navy
>
> From: U.S. Embassy, Bangkok, Thailand
>
> Office of the Coordinator, Orderly Departure Program
>
> Twenty-seven-year-old Vietnamese woman, identified as Nguyen Thi Lung, has tentatively identified you as a close friend and foster father. Subject resides in My Tho, People's Republic of Vietnam. Pending positive identification, it is possible she may qualify for status as refugee under Orderly Departure Program. Please advise. Colin ODP.

It was real. Lung had survived and somehow smuggled word out. I was stunned. During the years since Tet, I had nurtured a sensation that the story was perhaps not finished, but there had been little I could do to try to confirm her whereabouts or that she was even alive. For the next few weeks, I waited for more news. Then I received a letter from Donald Colin. He requested that I gather any evidence I might have to prove Lung's true identity, since she had taken a new name. Previously, the ODP list contained only the names of proven Amerasian children and Vietnamese who could document a previous close working relationship with Americans. According to the State Department, there was no precedent for a case such as Lung's, which depended on a vague relationship with American forces. Lung's situation was not covered by the ODP agreement. At the time, the Vietnamese government was cooperating only sporadically, and the ODP refugee negotiating process often stalled for long periods when the Vietnamese side simply stopped talking. It was just six years after the fall of South Vietnam, and the massive exodus of the boat people was seriously eroding the communist image.

The initial elation brought by Lung's letter gave way to a creeping dread that her years of persistence might prove to be in vain, and that her story might disappear in the abyss of bureaucracy, lost in the shuffle of tens of thousands of scrambling refugees. Lung's claim to a close American tie was tentative, and could be rejected by authorities on either or both sides. In desperation, I contrived a spectrum of moves to find Lung, which ranged from going to look for her in Vietnam to sending a proxy. It was still prohibited for an American serviceman to visit Vietnam unofficially.

While waiting impatiently, I worked closely with the ODP directors and complied with their request for photos and other data to establish Lung's identity. Luckily I found photos of her taken with me in my river patrol uniform and copies of the photo of Roderick Davis and me with Lung which had appeared in several New York newspapers. The photo that Lung had kept and then smuggled out of My Tho in Mr. Ha's letter was from a New York Daily News article, which showed her with Roderick Davis and me a few days after her release from the Saigon hospital in 1967. The picture had been taken by the UPI correspondent we had met that year at the restaurant in Saigon. In that photo, the last four letters of my name-tag showed clearly on my uniform—*usen*. Lung had always called me just the Vietnamese name of my rank, Dai Ui. In fact, she had never known my full name. Nevertheless, I confirmed Lung's identity using all the material I could find.

The intervention by the compassionate UPI correspondent, Sylvana Foa, soon changed the entire course of events. Sylvana was still a correspondent in Hong Kong. After reading Lung's remarkable letter, Sylvana mobilized her enigmatic network of friends and contacts in Vietnam to work on Lung's behalf. After two years of coordinating with the State Department's Orderly Departure Program in Bangkok and Washington, Sylvana's efforts paid off. Lung's name miraculously worked its way to the top of the Orderly Departure list for evacuation. Through Sylvana's frequent intercession with Don Colin from the ODP in Bangkok and Hal Foster of the Pacific Stars and Stripes, Lung was finally scheduled to depart Vietnam on a flight to Manila in early 1985.

Lung

Mr. Ha's letter triggered a series of events that spread over an eighteen month period. In January of 1985, two days before my scheduled departure from Vietnam, I rode to Saigon on a bus. Trang was sitting on my lap, Mr. Ha beside me as we rode out of My Tho. I said a quiet good-bye to the weeping tree as we drove past the Victory Hotel. I felt a little sad at leaving everything behind, but the excitement of travel was wonderful, and the thrill of the unknown future even greater. Where was I headed? Would I find Dai Ui? What would happen to Trang and me? I had no answers to these questions, but somehow I was confident, for I had seen a dream, the same one at least three times in succession, and it was a happy dream.

"Lung, remember above all what I told you about the children of Vietnam," Mr. Ha said, as we drove north on the dusty Highway 4. "Wherever you finally settle, your loyalties should be first to young Trang and then to your family here. You will start a new life. You will go as far as you are able, but you will always be Vietnamese." We parted at the airport, and as I watched the old man fade into the crowd, I believed he was surely an angel.

Gruff officials wearing sun helmets and khaki uniforms made us stand in endless lines. After hours of waiting, as I began to wonder if I was really going to leave, a group of officials approached the line. With them was a foreign looking man wearing a straw hat and a white suit, the kind Mr. Hamilton from the American Embassy had always worn. "You, what is your name?" I froze in fear. Was I going to be punished finally for having changed my name? Would I be taken away? Would Trang go with me? The man in white opened a folder and shuffled through some papers. He pointed to us, said something in a loud American voice. The other officials wandered off, as the man in white, who seemed to be suffering from the heat, guided us toward the airplane, ahead of the rest of the crowd. I did not look back.

We flew to the Philippines where we stayed in a crowded refugee camp for six months. There I met Miss Sylvana Foa, the author of the first letter answering Mr. Ha. She had located Dai Ui Peter through a series of articles placed with the old photo in several Far Eastern newspapers. She had contacted Dai Ui at first by telegram, then by telephone. He agreed to sponsor us to America.

Peter

Sylvana traveled to the Philippines and found Lung and Trang in the Refugee Processing Center in Marong, Bataan. She called me immediately afterwards and filled in the details for a story she had written for UPI. Sylvana was instrumental in obtaining Lung's exit from the camp six months later, and arranging her further travel to the U.S. as a war refugee.

On June 5, 1985, I received a call from Sylvana informing me that Lung and her daughter, Trang, would arrive at National Airport the following week. I was delighted and called Bob Donovan, my former executive officer from the patrol section 513 in Sa Dec. Bob agreed to come south from Bath, Maine to be with me when Lung arrived. I was unable to locate Roderick Davis.

Bob and I drove to National Airport in the muggy June afternoon. A reporter and photographer from a local Virginia newspaper joined us at the airport. We waited at the ramp as the rain turned to steam on the hot asphalt of the apron.

"The air reminds me a little of the delta," Bob said as we watched a United Airlines DC-9 roll through the light rain toward the dock.

"Add the smell of burning charcoal and nuc mam, and you'd have it," I answered. "Why do the smells remind us more than anything else of that time?"

"Probably 'cause the scents there were so unique, and so closely related to everything we did. Remember the aroma that hung around the old ladies when we searched the sampans?"

"Yeah, betel nut and the tobacco from the French Gauloise cigarettes."

"I think the worst was the smell in the hospitals."

"Bob, nothing was like the awful stench of death. I could smell it after every firefight—a putrid sweet smell."

"Pete," Bob looked at me, "we were damn lucky to have survived, I know, but this Lung thing is incredible. Who'd ever have thought we'd see her again—especially after Tet and with all the thousands of refugees milling around during the evacuation in '75, then the boat people. How the hell did she find us again?" He shook his head.

"I don't know, it's uncanny; they—the Viet children I mean—were always amazing."

"Yeah. I remember how they never showed emotion, just kind of took it on the chin." Bob suddenly pointed to the door of the ramp which had just swung open. Passengers began to pour out of the aircraft. A nervous feeling gripped my stomach. I felt like I was going on stage, or going out on a scary night patrol up a small canal. I had not felt the grip of fear in a long time. I was unsure how I would react when I saw Lung. She had been eleven when I last saw her in Sa Dec—just before Tet.

A United Airlines stewardess emerged, leading two small figures up the sloping ramp. One was small, the other even smaller. I recognized Lung as she walked with the stewardess. She was beautiful. Her childlike features had remained with her. She smiled broadly and continued closer. "Hello, Dai Ui," she said in a tiny voice, as if we had parted yesterday. "How are you?" she whispered in hesitant English. I was speechless.

Bob reached down and picked up Trang who, although skinny as a rail, had her mother's clear wide eyes. I was sure Bob stooped to hide his face from the correspondent's camera; his eyes had filled with tears.

Lung took several steps. I noticed she had a slight limp. Her plastic leg was the same one she had received in Saigon seventeen years earlier. She collapsed in my arms.

After adjusting to life in the northern Virginia suburbs, Lung and Trang began planning their new lives in America. Within weeks, Lung was receiving mail from a web of Vietnamese cousins, uncles, and other obscure relatives. She received job offers from several communities of Vietnamese in the South, Mid-West, and in nearby Virginia. Many Americans responded to the article in the local Fairfax newspaper which told Lung's story. Many called or wrote, offering her jobs as a seamstress or in embroidery, the specialty she had learned during her years with the Catholic sisters. The cold weather hurt Lung's upper leg, and she decided to move to the milder climate of San Diego, where she accepted a job as a seamstress, embroidering for a small cottage industry.

Just before they left, I invited some out-of-town guests to tour Washington. On a beautiful spring Sunday, Lung, Trang, and the visitors left for Washington. Lung put on her traditional au-dai, which she liked to wear when going out.

I had been to the Vietnam War Memorial only once before, to find the names of some of those lost from the river patrol force. Neither the guests nor Lung had ever seen the memorial. We parked along Constitution Avenue and strolled by the reflecting pool toward the Lincoln Memorial, then angled across the grass and approached the memorial from the direction of the statue of the four soldiers. As we neared the memorial, I noticed a clutch of men wearing camouflage fatigues hovering around the grounds. Some wore jungle hats, some berets of assorted colors. Few wore full uniform; instead they wore half uniforms, half grubby looking civilian clothing. Many sported beards. I grew concerned, and wondered what might happen bringing a Vietnamese woman into a situation which was often charged with emotion.

We first stopped and observed the statue. I watched Lung, who held Trang's hand tightly. Lung gazed up at the faces of the bronze soldiers, and then at me as she gradually absorbed the meaning of the memorial. Her English was still shaky. I explained, "Lung, this is the official memorial to the Americans who served and were lost in Southeast Asia." Lung nodded. We continued toward the black wall of names. As we walked closer, Lung hung back, and then retreated slightly to a grassy rise in the distance, indicating she did not want to come closer. She gazed at the flags and flowers scattered at the foot of the gleaming wall of names.

"You go, Dai Ui, your family," she said. The Vietnamese had specific customs of honoring the dead, always family related and strictly observed. I continued with the group, and then noticed two young men, one in a business suit, jacket slung over his shoulder, collar open, tie loosened, standing with head bowed before the wall. The second wore a green beret and camouflaged trousers. Both were pointing out names. The man in the suit stooped down, and inserted a small American flag into the ground before the wall, stepped back abruptly and saluted. The man in the green beret saluted too. The two men turned and walked away from the wall.

Both men seemed to notice Lung at the same time. She stood about ten yards away on the green slope slightly above them. The wind stirred her yellow au-dai, showing her white silk trousers and legs of different size. The two men appeared to be taken aback initially, stopped and blinked, as if seeing an apparition. The men's faces showed smeared tears, their eyes red. After a brief pause, the man in the green beret took several slow steps toward Lung, raised his left hand in which was clutched another small American flag. He beckoned deliberately to Lung, and held out the flag which fluttered in the wind. Lung paused, then stepped toward the two men. She tripped almost imperceptibly, then recovered her poise immediately, giving some doubt to the observer whether she had really tripped at all, or had made a graceful curtsey. She then raised her hands, and placed the palms together. A small crowd gathered around the two veterans and the two small Vietnamese figures. The veteran holding out the flag to Lung took another step forward. "Here, for you." He stood still holding the small flag out. Lung remained in the same position, head slightly bowed. Both veterans stood together quietly for a time watching Lung. She looked up, slowly extended her right hand, and accepted the flag. A helicopter approached from south of the Potomac River. The beating sounds of its blades made the familiar *thwock*, *thwock*, growing louder and louder. It passed overhead toward the White House, then faded in the distance. Lung looked up at the helicopter as it passed, then at the two veterans. When the sound died, she said softly, first in Vietnamese, "Cam on," and then in heavily accented English, "Thank you." Lung then glided forward toward the wall, her limp barely noticeable. As she stepped forward, the crowd parted before her, and she moved to the spot where the two men had been standing. She bent down and placed the flag next to theirs, slowly straightened, stepped back, put her palms together again, fingers pointing up, and bowed her head—the ancient Vietnamese sign of reverence.

Postscript

In early 1994, Lung and her daughter, Trang, returned to Ben Tre to visit her mother and surviving brothers. Mr. Ha had died sometime in the late 1980s. Lung's cousin, Din, still lives in My Tho. Her cousin, Phuong, lives in San Diego. Colonel Chuk, a paraplegic, was reportedly seen in a re-education camp in 1975. Cong, Co Thuong, and Sergeant Dinh were never heard from again. Minh, a surviving member of the delta river police, resides in My Tho. Yen, the nurse from the rehabilitation hospital, was never seen again, although there are rumors she is in California. During the period between April of 1967 and April of 1968, Sa Dec-based River Patrol Section 513 suffered ten percent casualties, including killed, wounded, and missing in action. Seaman David G. Ouellet, a gunner from our River Patrol Section 532 in My Tho, was awarded the Congressional Medal of Honor posthumously in 1967 for deflecting a hand grenade thrown into a PBR from the riverbank by a VC guerrilla, and then shielding his shipmates from the blast. The U.S. Delta River Patrol Force, Task Force 116, was awarded two Presidential Unit Citations, one for actions during the Tet Offensive.